PAST & PRESENT

History of the Foods We Eat;
Recipes Inspired by the Stories

Linda Lum

DEDICATION

Bill, Beth, and Megan,
your encouragement, support, and love
are a part of this history, and
the soul of this story.

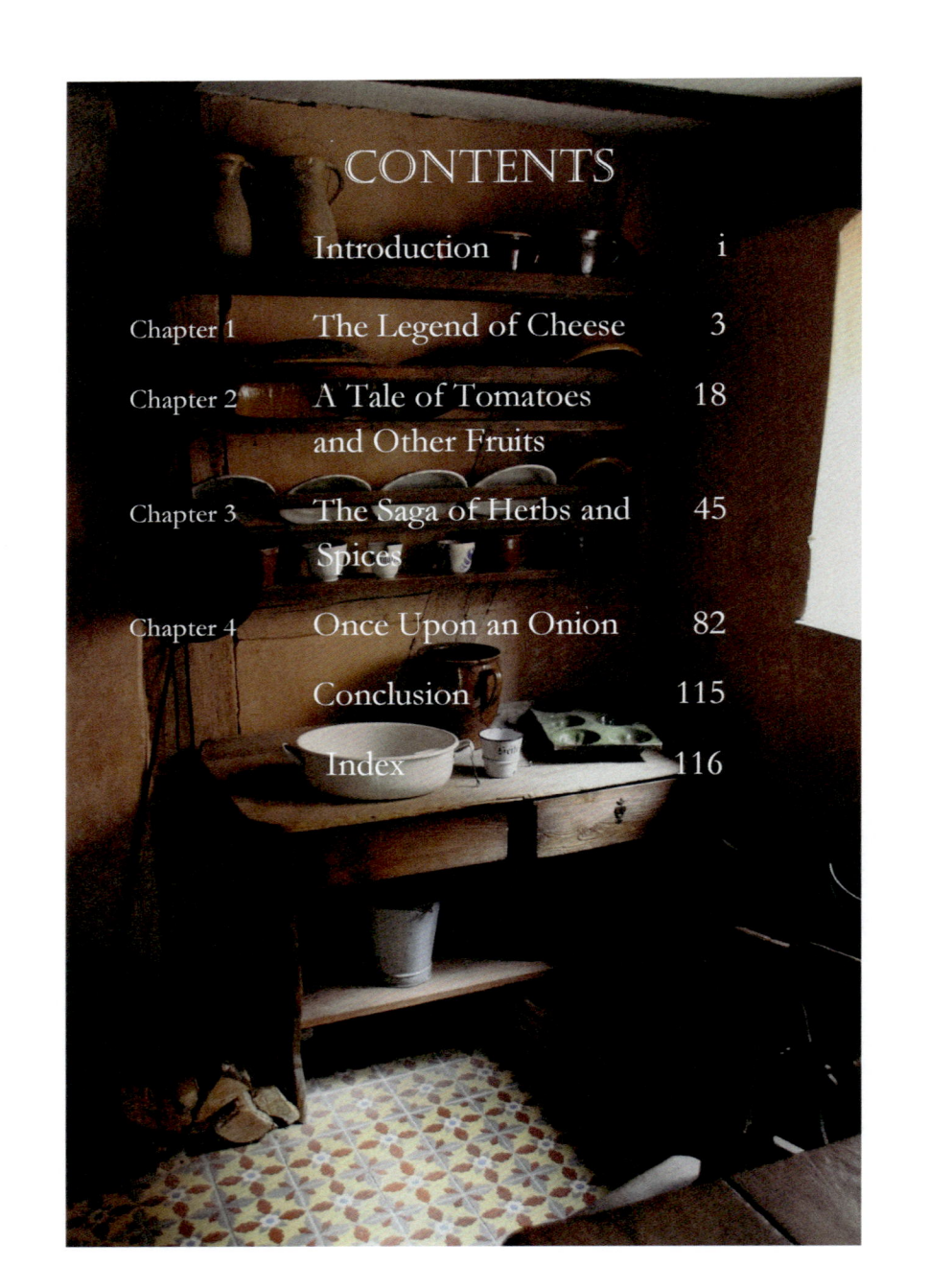

CONTENTS

INTRODUCTION

It is said that no two people are alike. Billions of souls have inhabited our planet, each one possessing their own unique beliefs and viewpoints, loves and desires. Despite our differences, there are two activities shared by all of us which are central, actually **vital** to our being—our first response when delivered from the womb is to breath, the next is to eat.

Yet eating is far more than simple sustenance. Food is how we relate with others. At a shared table, families tell stories of day-to-day events, but they also connect—children learn, relationships are nurtured, memories are shared and dreams blossom.

Food is present when we celebrate milestones—births, graduations, and weddings; it is comfort to the bereaved and a lifeline to the sick and needy. Eating is the common denominator of mankind, the one activity in which we share a mutual bond.

When prepared with care food can be magic—a true case of the whole exceeding the sum of its parts. Food is an art form, a fusion of tastes and textures that spans centuries of time. We may be separated by culture and continent, but food is the language that unites us all. Food is a part of who we are and what we have been; it is our history.

Food has a story to tell.

Photography – All photographs are by the author,
or were obtained from Pixabay.com under the
Creative Commons CC0 License (Public Domain)

Cover design by Linda Lum

THE LEGEND OF CHEESE

BLUE CHEESE

"A cheese may disappoint. It may be dull, it may be naive, it may be over sophisticated. Yet it remains; cheese, milk's leap toward immortality."— **Clifton Fadiman** *(American writer, editor and New Yorker book reviewer)*

The true origin of blue cheese has generated more than its fair share of folklore, speculation, and controversy. Italians claim that Gorgonzola is one of the world's oldest blue-veined cheeses, originating around 847 A.D. from a town of the same name. This spot, east of Milan, is in the northern region of Lombardy on the alpine border with Switzerland—an idyllic grazing area for cows.

It is said that centuries ago there was a young man in Italy, a cheese apprentice. It was springtime and a woodland nymph lured him away from his duties. Oh how romantic! Distracted by love, he left his cheese curds unattended overnight (oops!). To hide his oversight, the next morning he mixed the forgotten curds with fresh; however, a few weeks later the compromised batch began to turn blue. The mistake could no longer be hidden, but as luck would have it, this blunder proved to be a happy accident; Gorgonzola was born….or something like that. (Oddly enough, the French have a similar story for the creation of Roquefort).

The story of blue (or bleu) cheese doesn't end in Italy. One of the most popular tavern treats of the past few years has become Buffalo wings with blue cheese dressing. I don't know if the advent of this brew pub treat had an impact on the popularity of blue cheese, but it was certainly my introduction to the funky fromage. Until then I had assumed that blue (or bleu) cheese was only favored by those who dined on fancy European cuisine. In my opinion you can keep the buffalo wings—I'll just dive into the bowl of sauce.

Creamy Blue Cheese Sauce

<u>Ingredients</u>
1/2 cup buttermilk (see note below)
1/2 cup sour cream
1/2 cup mayonnaise
2 tsp. lemon juice
1 glove garlic, minced
1/8 tsp. black pepper
3/4 cup crumbled Danish blue or Stilton

<u>Directions</u>
Combine all ingredients except the cheese in a bowl and stir to blend. Fold in the crumbled blue cheese. If you prefer a smooth dressing, process everything in a blender or food processor. If the mixture seems too thick add a few more tsp. of milk.

NOTE: If you don't have buttermilk, don't worry. Place 1/2 tsp. of white vinegar in a 1 cup measuring cup. Fill to the 1/2 cup mark with regular milk, stir and let sit for 5 minutes.

The inspiration for this next recipe came from Better Homes and Gardens. Their website has a 'triple Tomato Soup" with just two comments—one reviewer loved it, but didn't stick to the recipe. The other followed the recipe and complained that it was "bland." I didn't make their recipe, but slapped on my Sherlock Holmes cap to find a solution to ramping up flavor without increasing calories.

My first rule is "always use the best ingredients". If you use canned tomatoes, use the best ones you can find—not the generic bottom-price variety. Secondly, use fresh herbs whenever possible. And my last rule is **think** about your cooking technique. Is there some way of encouraging more flavors out of these ingredients? My Sherlock Holmes powers of deduction led me to investigate the tomatoes. They contain lots of natural sugars so why not caramelize them in the oven? Here is the Carb Diva approach to "Tomato Soup to the 3rd Power."

Triple Tomato Soup

<u>Ingredients</u>
2 14-oz. cans diced tomatoes
2 tablespoons olive oil, divided
1 large onion, diced
1/2 cup celery, diced
2 cloves garlic, minced
3/4 cup sundried tomatoes, (not oil packed)
1/2 of a 6-oz. can tomato paste
1 14-oz. can chicken or vegetable broth
1 tablespoon fresh sage, minced
1 bay leaf
2 tablespoons fresh parsley, minced
2 tsp. lemon juice
1/2 cup Bavarian (or blue of your choice)

<u>Directions</u>
1) Preheat oven to 450 degrees F.

2) Strain canned tomatoes, reserving juices. Spread canned tomatoes on large baking sheet; season with salt and pepper to taste. Drizzle with 1 tablespoon olive oil. Roast in oven about until caramelized, about 30 minutes.

3) Meanwhile, sauté onion, celery, and garlic in large saucepan, with the remaining 1 tablespoon olive oil, until softened, about 10 minutes.

4) Add the roasted canned tomatoes, reserved tomato juices, sun-dried tomatoes, broth, sage, and bay leaf. Simmer until vegetables are very tender, about 20 minutes.

5) Remove bay leaf. Puree soup in pot with immersion blender until smooth. Stir in chopped parsley and lemon juice. Taste and adjust seasoning as needed. Garnish with crumbled cheese.

Potato Gnocchi with Gorgonzola Sauce

Ingredients

1 1/3 cups instant mashed potato flakes

1 1/3 cups boiling water

1 tsp. salt

2 large eggs

3 cups sifted all-purpose flour

3/4 cup heavy cream

1/2 cup crumbled Gorgonzola

Bread crumbs (for garnish)

Good-quality olive oil

Fresh basil, minced (optional)

Directions

1) Place the mashed potato flakes in a large mixing bowl and cover with the boiling water. Stir just to moisten and let sit for about 10 minutes. Add the salt and 2 eggs and beat on low speed with mixer until smooth. Add the flour and beat just until the flour is incorporated and the dough is smooth. Don't overmix—that will make the gnocchi tough. Allow the dough to rest for 30 minutes. Then bring a large pot of water to boil over medium-high heat.

2) Lightly spray the inside of a pastry bag with non-stick cooking spray (such as Pam). Do NOT place a decorating tip in the pastry bag—use just the bag and coupler.

3) Spoon your potato gnocchi "dough" into the pastry bag. With one hand gently squeeze the bag to gradually force the potato dough to the tip of the bag. With your other hand, cut off the dough with a sharp knife. Continue to squeeze and cut, allowing the dough to drop into your pot of water.

4) Using this method you can form and cook your gnocchi very quickly and without added flour.

5) Bring cream to a simmer over medium-low heat in large sauté pan. Add cheese and cook, stirring constantly, until Gorgonzola is melted. Add cooked gnocchi to the pan and toss to coat. Place gnocchi in oven-safe dish. Sprinkle bread crumbs on top; drizzle with olive oil and top with basil. Broil 5 inches from heat until bubbly and crumbs are browned. Watch carefully so that the crumbs don't burn!

BRIE

"Now on that day, being the sixth day of the week, he was not willing to eat the flesh of beast or bird. The bishop, being by reason of the nature of the place unable to procure fish immediately, ordered some excellent cheese, white with fat, to be placed before him. Charles…required nothing else, but taking up his knife and throwing away the mold, which seemed to him abominable, he ate the white of the cheese. Then the bishop, who was standing nearby like a servant, drew close and said…

"Why do you do that, lord Emperor? You are throwing away the best part." On the persuasion of the bishop, Charles… put a piece of the mold in his mouth and slowly ate it and swallowed it like butter. Then, approving the bishop's advice, he said "Very true, my good host," and he added, "Be sure to send me every year two cartloads of such cheeses."

*— Quoted from a biography of **Charlemagne** by a monk at a monastery in the late 9th century.*

Charlemagne (also known as Charles the Great) was a medieval emperor, the king of the Franks, a Germanic tribe in what is now Belgium. He ruled much of Western Europe and was committed to uniting all of his peoples into one kingdom and bringing them under Christian rule.

According to legend, Charlemagne fell in love with a certain cheese when he first dined on it at a monastery east of Paris. (Lovers of Roquefort will claim the cheese to be theirs, but I strongly disagree!)

Unlike other cheeses of the area, the name brie is not protected — "brie" can be used by anyone, but a true 'tastes-like-it-should' brie must be made in the place where it originated – the Seine-et-Marne.

Or so we have been led to believe. There is another legend, a legend that takes us far away, to the east and south of France, long before Charlemagne, long before the monks. 'The History of Brie" as told at ehow.com explains that:

…the earliest form of Brie was purportedly created by accident in the Middle East. The story goes that a nomad filled his saddlebag with milk before embarking on a long horseback journey. His animal carcass saddlebag was lined with rennet (an enzyme also called rennin or chymosin) and the combination with the milk created a watery liquid (whey) and solid, white lumps (curds) that was an ancestor, perhaps, of the first Brie.

Whether as an accident in the saddle bag of a hapless wanderer, or the brainchild of Frankish monks, the popularity of brie extended far beyond the borders of France. It's rumored that King Henry IV of England was introduced to brie by his wife, Queen Margot. So taken was he by the bloomy cheese that when given the choice of the company of his mistress or dining with Margot, he resided with the cheese.

The cheese of kings became the king of cheeses in the 19th century. According to www.pongcheese.co.uk:

At one of history's most superior banquets, the Congress of Vienna, the 19th-century French diplomat Talleyrand reportedly called for a break from divvying up the nations, following the fall of the French Empire, in order to stage a cheese contest. More than sixty varieties of cheese were brought together, which were all tasted with great attention. Lord Castlereagh represented the English with Stilton, Dutch minister Baron de Falck nominated Limberger, Italy presented Strachino and Switzerland put forward Gruyere to name but a few. Duke de Talleyrand remained quiet until the end, when the Brie was brought in. After a vote they all praised French gastronomy and maintained that there was no other cheese that matched up to the Brie de Meaux and declared a new king "Le Roi des Fromages" (King Of Cheeses).

Brie is a cheese as rich in flavor as it is in history. Here is how to create two brie appetizers that are "fit for a king".

Brie and Fruit

This is absolutely a marriage made in (cheese) Heaven. Brie longs for a partner, it sighs with deep yearning for a soul mate. Tangy, earthy, buttery brie was made to be served with fruit. Well, not all fruits. As with the blue cheeses (or any cheese for that matter) I would avoid citrus or any fruit that is greatly acidic. But if you have oozy brie looking for a partner, you might consider one (or more) of these:

. strawberries
. fresh or dried figs
. apple
. pear
. blueberries or blackberries
. fresh or dried apricots

And, while you are in the snacking mood, what about a whole-grain cracker? Add a grain to your fruit and cheese and you have a wonderful mid-day meal.

Brie in Puff Pastry

Ingredients
1 sheet of puff pastry, thawed (I like Pepperidge Farms)
1 10-12 ounce round of brie
1 egg PLUS 1 tsp. water, beaten (this is an egg wash "glue" to hold things together and make a pretty shellac)
Goodies (see list on next page!)

Directions
1) Preheat oven to 400 degrees F.

2) Line a rimmed baking sheet with parchment paper and set aside.

3) Roll out puff pastry on lightly-floured surface to a square about 11 inches by 11 inches. Place your round of brie in the center of the pastry, and then top it with your choice of "goodies".

4) Bring the sides/edges of the pastry up over the brie to form a neat package. You want to totally encase the brie in the pastry. Brush a bit of the beaten egg over the edges to seal.

5) Place the brie onto the parchment-lined baking sheet Brush a bit more egg wash on the brie package (top and sides, but don't let it "puddle" on the baking sheet). Bake until the package is browned, about 35 to 40 minutes.

6) This is the most difficult part of all. Employ extreme patience and allow this amazing treat to sit for about 10 minutes. Trust me — your brie cheese will still be hot and amazing, but not like **lava**.

Goodies for the brie package:

Sweet
honey
dried fruit (cranberries, sliced figs, apricots, apples)
cranberry sauce
raspberry or blackberry jam
orange marmalade
cherry, apricot, or peach preserves

crunchy
chopped nuts (walnuts, pecans, slivered almonds)
candied walnuts or pecans

savory
sautéed mushrooms
mango chutney (I like Major Grey's)
crisp cooked crumbled bacon
oil-packed dried tomatoes
caramelized onions

PARMESAN

"If anyone ever tells you that you put too much Parmesan cheese on your pasta, stop talking to them. You don't need that kind of negativity in your life." –Anon.

For this story, we need to travel across soil and century, following the natural rhythm of the seasons, to Italy, 1,300 A.D. Today we know this area as Parma and Reggio Emilia. In the 12th century it was the heart of a Benedictine monk community where life was dedicated to worship, study, and self-subsistence. When not in prayer and devotion, the monks tended gardens and orchards, milled grain, baked bread, and raised livestock for meat and butter.

And, they were making cheese, but not just any cheese. The monks were using the milk of Vacche Rosso cows, cows grazing in the perfect climate that supports the lush grasses between the Rhine and Po Rivers. And the monks discovered a method to create a low moisture (grana) cheese that would not only keep well, but would improve with age.

They still use the milk from farms in this fertile, green area—about 4,000 of them today. No preservatives or chemical additives are used to hurry the process—only whey, natural rennet, and salt are blended with the milk. The only significant change in technique from centuries past is that cows no longer graze in pastures. Instead, the grasses are grown and fed to them in barns; this insures careful food intake monitoring and thus, a consistent product.

And to insure that this treasured product continues to be consistent, a consortium was established in 1934. This group brought all producers together to establish production standards and to safeguard and promote the name. Today all cheeses bearing the fire-brand mark PARMIGIANO REGGIANO have been made according to the strict *Disciplinare di Produzione* (Production Specifications) and checked by the consortium's experts. Only cheeses that pass inspection can be fire-branded.

The creation of Parmigiano is a fascinating process. Whole milk from the morning milking is blended with skimmed milk from the previous evening's milking. (Even this skimming process is done naturally—the milk is held in vats and allowed to separate). The whole milk/skim milk blend is then pumped into copper-lined vats. Whey and rennet are added, and the milk curdles and separates. Fire is then brought into the picture; the copper vats are heated to 55 degrees C. and the cheese granules form and sink to the bottom of the vat. After resting for 30 minutes, the cheese is removed by the cheese maker, divided in two, wrapped in muslin, and placed in a mold which gives it its final characteristic shape. At this point each wheel weighs about 100 pounds.

After two days a plastic belt imprinted numerous times with the Parmigiano-Reggiano name, the plant's number, and the month and year of production is put around the cheese. This imprint becomes a distinct and unique part of the cheese—a fingerprint of sorts. Next comes a brine bath of 20 to 25 days, and then the slow aging process begins. The cheese wheels (each one made from 600 liters of milk) are laid out in long rows in maturation rooms. These wheels rest on wooden tables where the outsides dry, allowing a natural (perfectly edible) crust to form. The minimum maturation time is twelve months, and only after that length of time can it be decided if each individual cheese is worthy of the name it was given at its birth.

A cheese as beautifully crafted as Parmigiano (Parmesan) is worthy of thoughtful pairing with quality ingredients. It deserves to be more than a simple dusting atop a mound of pasta cloaked with jarred spaghetti sauce. My first recipe uses greens freshly harvested from my backyard. For some, these plants are a nuisance; to me they are the herald of springtime. I've travelled to almost every corner of the United States. Each area has its own unique beauty, but nowhere else have I found the diversity of plants that are here in my little corner of the world. My husband and I own a tiny little piece of the "Evergreen State"—one and one-half acres in the Puget Sound region. When we bought our property years ago, it was engulfed in a tangle of ferns, huckleberries, and briars. Twenty-five years later one acre has been pretty much 'tamed"—wild berries and weeds have been replaced by shrubs, perennials and annual flowers. But the "back" one-half acre is still forested and wild. A nature trail meanders through that section of our property, providing an amazing display of native plants—huckleberries, ferns, trillium, and numerous wildflowers. We are so blessed to be here.

However, there is one rather unwelcome plant that raises its ugly little head each Spring—the stinging nettle. For the unaware or uninitiated, stinging nettles are a beautiful plant, but their stems and leaves are covered with millions of tiny hairs—each hair, at the merest brush, ready to release a painful dose of formic acid. The sting causes extreme pain and welts that can last anywhere from several hours to several days.

Well, guess what I did today? I harvested nettles!! Yes, call me crazy, but these denizens of the forest are wonderfully tasty and nutritious if you know how to conquer their "wild side". A brief simmer in boiling water is all that is needed to tame the beast and have a nutritious deep green vegetable ready to be sautéed, simmered in soup, or turned into a rich pesto. (I wonder what brave soul first attempted to eat them.)

Spring Harvest Pesto

Ingredients
2 quarts of stinging nettles, cooked per instructions and squeezed dry—to equal about 1 cup
1/2 cup walnuts
3 garlic cloves
1/4 cup grated Parmesan cheese
3/4 cup olive oil

<u>Directions</u>

1) You MUST wear protective gloves when harvesting nettles. Not canvas or cotton—something non-absorbent such as vinyl or cowhide. Snip just the top part (or first three levels) of leaves and place in a clean bucket. Keep clipping until your bucket is full. Bring your harvest into the kitchen.

2) Bring a large pot of water to boil. Don a clean pair of rubber gloves and place you nettles into the kitchen sink. Run a bit of water over your harvest and then begin plucking leaves from the plants. Place the leaves in a colander and discard the stems. Scoop the leaves into the boiling pot of water. Set your timer for 3 minutes, and stir the pot once or twice so that all of the leaves are submerged in the boiling water.

3) After 3 minutes drain the cooked nettle leaves into a colander and let cool. When cool enough to handle, squeeze the water out of the cooked nettles (yes, they are now safe to touch). Give them a rough chop on your cutting board; now you're ready to make pesto.

4) Place the prepared nettles, walnuts, garlic, and parmesan in a food processor. Whir until finely chopped. While the blade is moving slowly pour in the olive oil. Stop and taste your pesto. You'll probably need to add a bit of salt. If the mixture seems too thick, add some water (about 2 tablespoons).

Risotto—no discussion of Parmesan is complete without mention of this luxurious Italian side dish. Toothsome Arborio rice is simmered in broth to a creamy richness, and as the dish is completed Parmesan cheese is deftly folded in, its nutty, salty flavor providing a perfect contrast to sweet, silky mascarpone.

Mushroom Risotto

<u>Ingredients</u>

2 tablespoons unsalted butter
1 1/2 tsp. olive oil
1/2 cup minced onion
1 garlic clove, minced
1/2 pound fresh mushrooms, sliced
1/2 tsp. dried thyme leaves
3/4 cup dry white wine
1 cup Arborio rice
1/4 tsp. black pepper
3-4 cups chicken, vegetable, or mushroom broth, heated to a simmer
1/4 cup Parmigiano-Reggiano, grated
1/4 cup mascarpone cheese

Directions

1) In large sauté pan melt 1 tablespoon butter with olive oil over medium heat. Add onion and garlic and cook until onion is soft, about 2 minutes. Stir in mushrooms and cook until lightly browned (3 to 4 minutes). Stir in thyme. Add 1/4 cup of the wine and cook until wine is absorbed. Remove from heat and cover to keep warm.

2) Melt remaining 1 tablespoon butter in a large heavy saucepan over medium heat. Add rice, pepper, and remaining 1/2 cup white wine. Stir to insure that rice does not clump together and cook until wine is absorbed. Add 1 cup broth; reduce heat to low, and stir until broth is almost absorbed. Continue to add broth, 1/2 cup at a time and stirring until rice is creamy and tender but still firm in center. This should take about 15 to 18 minutes.

3) Stir in mushrooms. Remove from heat and stir in Parmigiano-Reggiano and mascarpone cheese.

Why Arborio is Best

Long-grain white rice has a long, slender kernel 4 to 5 times as long as it is wide. This type of rice cooks fluffy, with separate grains—no stickiness.

Medium-grain white rice .has a shorter, wider kernel (two to three times longer than its width) than long grain rice. Cooked grains are more moist and tender, and have a greater tendency to cling together more than long grain rice.

Short-grain white rice .is short, round, plump, and a little bit sassy (just like me). Short-grain rices are not cooked like their long- or medium-grain cousins. First, the rice is gently sautéed in butter or olive oil so that each of the grains is coated. Next, a splash of wine is added to the pan; at this point the rice is stirred constantly until the wine has all but evaporated. Then the fun begins. Hot broth is added to the pan, one ladle-full at a time, and allowed to simmer into and be absorbed by the rice. This process is repeated until the rice is rich and creamy, but still holds its shape (test a grain with your teeth to see if it is done. You want al dente like "Goldilocks spaghetti"--not too hard, not to soft, but **just right**.

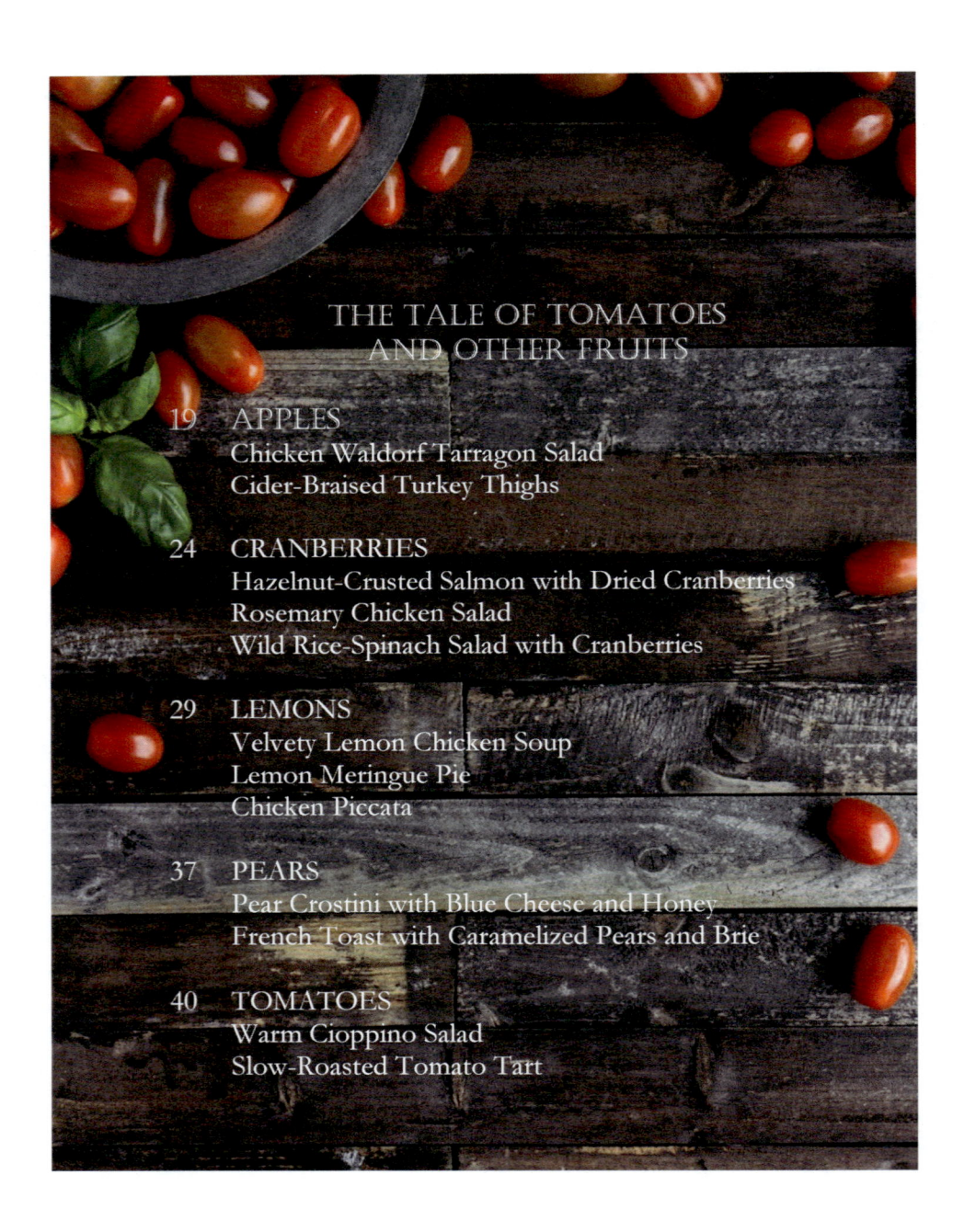

THE TALE OF TOMATOES AND OTHER FRUITS

APPLES

*"Even if I knew that tomorrow the world would go to pieces, I would still plant my apple tree." –**Martin Luther***

From the above quote, it's quite clear that Martin Luther loved apples, but they were grown long before that famous German monk planted his tree. Perhaps we should go back a bit further in history:

*"In order to make an apple pie from scratch, you must first invent the universe."—**Carl Sagan***

Too far? OK, let's compromise and begin our tale a few thousand years ago in Kazakhstan, near present day Alma-Ata, the "city of apples". Almost five centuries before the birth of Christ, the Silk Road passed through this place; one can assume that merchants enjoyed the fruits of those luscious apple trees, filled their pockets, and took seeds to their homelands.

Food historians tell us that at early as the 3rd century B.C. apples were cultivated by the Greeks and Romans. The Romans carried the seeds to the far reaches of their empire and, with the Norman conquest of 1066 A.D., apples were introduced to England from France as well.

Now fast-forward to the 17th century. European settlers to the land called America discovered that native crab apples were not to their liking. Unlike the sweet, crisp eating apples that we enjoy today, the crab apples were small and bitter. Nevertheless they made wonderful cider. (Fermented cider was appreciated not only because of the mild alcoholic buzz, but because it was safer than drinking the water.)

Settlers from Europe brought saplings and seeds from their homelands, but those first attempts at growing apples were less than "fruitful." The saplings (grafted stock) didn't survive the harsh, unfamiliar climate. But on the other hand, the seeds produced well. Years later, as Americans travelled west, they took those hardy apples with them and the rest, as they say, is history...

...or not. Another part of our first tale is how those apples have been used. I have two stories to share with you. The first takes place in New York City.

Once upon a time, there was a man named Oscar. He made a salad with celery, apples, and lettuce. And they lived happily ever after. The End. No, I'm joking. Here's the real story. Oscar Tschirky was the maître d'hôtel at the Waldorf Hotel (later to become the Waldorf-Astoria) in New York City. He made several signature dishes during his career, many of which appeared in the 1896 cookbook *"Oscar of the Waldorf"*. But the creation we still talk about (and enjoy) is the Waldorf Salad. The original didn't contain walnuts, but when *"Rector Cook Book"* was published in 1928, walnuts were added to the list of ingredients. Waldorf Salad became immensely popular; Cole Porter even mentioned it in his 1934 song *"You're the Top"*.

Today there are countless versions of the Waldorf Salad. Many add chicken or turkey, grapes, or dried fruits. A few cooks choose yogurt in place of mayonnaise. I have my own favorite twist on the original—Chinese cabbage replaces the original leaf lettuce and plain mayonnaise is upgraded to a homemade lemon mayonnaise. (Yes, I'm going to help you make real mayonnaise in your own kitchen!).

Chicken Waldorf Tarragon Salad

<u>Ingredients</u>
3 cups diced cooked chicken
1/2 cup celery heart, diced
1 cup diced apple
1/2 cup dried cranberries
4 tsp. minced fresh tarragon
1/2 cup smoked almonds,   finely chopped
1 cup **lemon mayonnaise**, (see recipe below)
1/4 tsp. salt
1/8 tsp. black pepper
2 cups Chinese cabbage, finely chopped

<u>Directions</u>
Combine all ingredients in a large mixing bowl. Cover and chill at least 30 minutes. Serve on chilled plates.

Lemon Mayonnaise

<u>Ingredients</u>
2 large egg yolks
1/4 tsp. salt
1 tablespoon lemon juice
3/4 cup olive oil
1 tsp. fresh lemon zest

<u>Directions</u>
Place the egg yolks, salt, and lemon juice in the bowl of a blender. Process until the egg yolk and juice are well-combined and the yolks begin to turn to a lighter shade of yellow. Remove the fill cap (central portion of the lid). Place the olive oil in a glass measuring cup with a lip suitable for pouring. With the blender running, begin adding the oil to the yolk/lemon juice mixture. Start with just one drop at a time and increase to a steady but very slow stream as the oil is absorbed. Stir in lemon zest.

I promised you two stories. This second one begins 3,000 miles away and about 42 years before Oscar tossed that famous salad. In 1854 Steilacoom became the first town incorporated in the State of Washington. That simple fact is central to this story for two reasons – Washington is the Number 1 producer of apples within the United States, **and** Steilacoom is where I live. In the little Town of Steilacoom (population 6,000) there is an annual event on the 1st Sunday of October—the Steilacoom Apple Squeeze. On that day, vintage apple cider presses are rolled out from storage and *pressed* into action.

Of course there is a lot more than cider happening. The entire downtown corridor of the town (two blocks) is closed to traffic and a fair of booths and displays lines both sides of the street. Apple pie and ice cream (with warm cinnamon sauce) is sold by the slice in Town Hall. The kids can enjoy pony rides, birdhouse building, face painting, and bouncy houses.

There are activities for the "big kids" as well—live local music, food vendors, craft demonstrations, experts to provide advice about your own apple tree (if you bring a leaf and an apple for identification), and apple cider floats. At the end of the day, our family is tired and hungry (that mile-long trek from downtown to our house is all uphill). So we need a hearty meal. And the focus, of course, is on apples.

Cider-Braised Turkey Thighs

<u>Ingredients</u>
4 turkey thighs
Salt and pepper to taste
4 slices thick-cut bacon, diced
2 tablespoons olive oil
3 carrots, pared and diced
1 medium yellow onion, diced
1 fresh bay leaf
3 fresh thyme sprigs
2 cups apple cider (not juice)
1 cup chicken broth

<u>Directions</u>

1) Preheat oven to 300 degrees F. Season turkey thighs with salt and pepper and set aside.

2) Sauté bacon in Dutch oven over medium heat until crisp, about 5 minutes. Remove from pan with slotted spoon and set aside. Add olive oil to the pan with the bacon drippings. Sauté the turkey thighs in the pan until browned, about 5 minutes per side. Do not crowd the pan—you want the turkey to brown, not steam. If necessary, cook in two batches. When browned, remove the turkey thighs to a plate and set aside.

3) Add the carrots and onion to the pan. Cook, stirring occasionally, until the carrots begin to brown and the onions are soft, about 5 minutes. Add the bay leaf, thyme, and cider. Bring to a boil, scraping up any browned bits on the bottom of the pan. Cook until reduced by half, about 5 minutes.

4) Stir in the chicken broth and return to a boil. Add the cooked bacon and the browned turkey thighs. Cover and place in preheated oven. Cook for about 45 minutes. Turn the turkey over so that the portion that was submerged in the cider/broth mixture is now on top. Return to the oven **without** the cover. Cook another 45 minutes, or until the turkey is tender.

CRANBERRIES

"There are some things in every country that you must be born to endure; and another hundred years of general satisfaction with Americans and America could not reconcile this expatriate to cranberry sauce, peanut butter, and drum majorettes." —**Alistair Cooke** *(British-born American journalist, well known as host of 'Masterpiece Theater' PBS*

Love it or hate it, cranberry sauce is a ubiquitous cast member of the traditional American Thanksgiving Day meal. Our childhood history lessons tell of Pilgrims and Native Americans dining together on pumpkins, rabbit, and cranberries. But long before the first Thanksgiving, cranberries were known and used across the Atlantic. The common cranberry of North America is the *Vaccinium oxycoccos*, but it has a smaller cousin (*Vaccinium microcarpum* or *Oxycoccus microcarpus)* in northern Europe. So it makes sense that the combination of savory, fatty meats (rabbit or turkey) with tart fruit (cranberries) would be a part of the Pilgrims' celebration. I'm sure you have heard of Swedish meatballs with lingonberry sauce, pork with applesauce, goose with cherries, duck a l'orange, and even fish with lemon—all common meat and fruit pairings.

But, back to the cranberry. In late November cooks throughout the United States would simmer whole berries with sugar to make cranberry sauce—the appearance of the cranberry was an annual event. That all changed however in 1987 when the Ocean Spray Company began marketing sweetened dried cranberries (craisins). Now, cranberries appear not only as sauce but in main dishes as well, and they are used the year around, not just in November.

I developed three recipes that feature craisins, and one of them was really the beginning of my culinary journey. My recipe collection contains dozens of dishes lovingly prepared by my mother. But to be honest mom was not an adventurous cook. Simple meat and potatoes and "normal" vegetables were served in our dining room. It wasn't until I moved away from home that I discovered the wonders of shellfish, couscous, mushrooms, and a wealth of vegetables (asparagus, broccoli, and Brussels sprouts to name a few). Once I broke away from the meat-and-potatoes framework, I started to really enjoy cooking; my new-found enthusiasm made me eager to share my experience with others. So I began to submit my "creations" to monthly magazines (Sunset, Cooking Light, and Better Homes and Gardens were a few) and to enter cooking contests.

The first recipe is one of my favorites because of its versatility. I developed the second recipe to add some unexpected flavors and textures to the traditional chicken salad. Most recipes call for celery, onion and (too much) mayonnaise. Greek yogurt replaces half of the traditional mayonnaise and provides a subtle tang. I like the pairing of sweet cranberries with the salty/savory chicken. If you don't care for rosemary you could omit it, but please don't leave out the smoked almonds. They are a surprise addition, and one for which I have never heard a complaint.

The third recipe was a winner in one of those cooking contests and my break away from meat and potatoes. The theme of the competition was to create a dish featuring local ingredients. Since I live in the Pacific Northwest salmon and hazelnuts were an obvious choice—both signatures of our region. You might think that mayonnaise is an odd partner with cooked salmon, but it keeps the flesh moist. The combination of citrus (lemon) with fish is as routine as peanut butter and jelly, so orange marmalade and zest seemed a natural addition. Hazelnuts provide a contrasting crunch. And this dish wouldn't be the same without the color and tangy taste of dried cranberries.

Wild Rice Spinach Salad with Cranberries

<u>Ingredients</u>
1 pkg. (10 oz.) frozen chopped spinach, thawed
3 cups cooked wild rice
2 cups cooked brown rice
1/2 cup slivered almonds, toasted
1/4 cup sliced green onions
4 slices turkey bacon, cooked crisp and crumbled
1 cup smoked turkey breast from the deli, diced
1 cup dried cranberries
Salad dressing (recipe below)

<u>Directions</u>
Squeeze as much water as possible from the thawed spinach. Place the spinach and all remaining ingredients in a large mixing bowl. Pour the dressing over the salad. Toss to combine. Cover and refrigerate.

Salad Dressing

<u>Ingredients</u>
1/2 cup olive oil
2 tablespoons rice wine vinegar
2 tablespoons soy sauce
1 tsp. honey
1/4 tsp. salt
1/4 tsp. black pepper

<u>Directions</u>
Whisk all ingredients together in small mixing bowl.

Wild Rice Salad Substitutions and Additions

. Cashews or walnuts can be used in place of the almonds
. Diced avocado
. Cooked garbanzo beans
. Shredded carrots
. Oil-packed sun dried tomatoes
. Snap peas
. Diced red bell pepper
. Fresh spinach or arugula

. Omit the bacon and turkey and substitute baked tofu or tempah to make this a vegetarian meal

Rosemary Chicken Salad Sandwich

Ingredients
3 cups cooked chicken, diced (I think white meat is best in this recipe)
1/2 cup celery, diced
1/2 cup dried cranberries
1/3 cup chopped smoked almonds
1 tsp. fresh rosemary, minced
2 tablespoons fresh chives
1/3 cup mayonnaise
1/3 cup plain Greek yogurt
1/2 tsp. salt
1/8 tsp. black pepper

Directions
Combine all ingredients in large mixing bowl. Cover and chill at least one hour to allow flavors to blend

Hazelnut-Crusted Salmon with Dried Cranberries

Ingredients

1 pound salmon filet, cut into 4 equal pieces
1/2 cup low-fat or fat-free mayonnaise
1 tablespoon orange marmalade
1/2 cup chopped hazelnuts
1/2 cup dried cranberries, rough chopped
2 tsp. minced fresh tarragon
1/2 tsp. orange zest
1/2 tsp. salt
1/4 tsp. ground black pepper

Directions

1) Preheat oven to 400 degrees F. Spray a rimmed baking sheet with non-stick cooking spray.

2) Place salmon pieces on baking sheet, skin-side down. Stir together mayonnaise and marmalade and spread equal amounts on each piece of salmon. Top with hazelnuts and dried cranberries. Sprinkle on tarragon, zest, salt, and pepper. Bake in preheated oven 12-15 minutes or until fish flakes easily with a fork

Fresh Cranberries 101 (or how to select and store the best)

The best cranberries are firm and plump, without wrinkles or blemish. Avoid berries that are pale—they should be bright to dark red in color.

After sorting (and removing any damaged or blemished berries), seal the "keepers" in a plastic bag. They have a long shelf life—up to 2 months in the refrigerator . For longer storage, toss that plastic bag into the freezer where your cranberries will remain perfectly happy (and happily perfect) for up to a year.

LEMONS

"When life gives you lemons…add melted butter, toasted paprika, and dip some lobster in it!" **–Stuart J. Scesney**

What is the stuff of your dreams? What images fill your daytime reverie or invade your thoughts during sleep? Perhaps you drift to far-away places—strolling on a white sand beach glistening below an azure sky; or maybe you envision hiking in a wildflower-strewn alpine meadow beneath sapphire-blue glaciers. I have a friend whose thoughts drift to sailing across a tranquil sea—destination nowhere. My husband's passion is pushing it to the limit on a switch-back road in his Miata (with the top down of course).

I dream of food, or more specifically, I dream of *cooking* food.

Imagine if you will, delicate cream scones—flaky, triangle-shaped breakfast pastries studded with fresh blueberries, adorned with crunchy sugar crystals, and drizzled with a citrus glaze. Or perhaps a luxurious creamy chicken soup with a refreshing hint of citrus. Maybe tender, boneless chicken cutlets dredged in flour and then quickly sautéed in butter until the interior is cooked to a moist perfection and the exterior is golden and crisp. A bright drizzle of butter caper sauce provides just the right balance of lush creaminess and briny zing.

Or you might be in the mood for something sweet. A luscious cream pie—the crust is buttery, flaky, and crisp. The filling is a bright yellow hue, sweet, tart, and creamy. Billowy, cloud-like puffs of egg white meringue cover the filling. And as an added bonus the meringue has been gently kissed by flame to impart a subtle golden color and crisp exterior to the soft egg white blanket.

Are you getting hungry yet? We've covered all of the bases—breakfast, lunch, dinner, and dessert. And what is the common thread? All of these are flavored with and enhanced by *lemon*. Is there any one food (other than bacon?) that appears in so many different types of foods and cuisines?

But once upon a time... lemon was nothing more than a pretty face.

In researching this topic, I learned that the lemon plant is extremely adaptable and hybridizes easily— that's good news (unless, of course, you are a food historian, so our legend of the lemon is brief). Some people think that the lemon was first cultivated in China; others believe it originated north of India, near Kashmir. The lemon tree gradually migrated to Southeast Asia, to the kingdom of the Medes, and to the Persian Empire. Persian merchants brought the lemon to Sicily, but it was little more than an ornamental plant. Despite its versatility (which we recognize and embrace today) cultivation of the lemon for culinary use didn't occur until the 15th century when lemons were used in Genoa to create a tart-tangy beverage. It was Christopher Columbus who brought lemons to the New World.

Now, let's start making those foods I tantalized you with at the start of this topic.

Velvety Lemon Chicken Soup

<u>Ingredients</u>
1 small lemon
3 cups good quality chicken stock
2 tablespoons unsalted butter
2 tablespoons flour
1/4 cup heavy cream
Garnish—2 tablespoons minced flat-leaf parsley

<u>Directions</u>
1) Cut two 2-inch strips of lemon peel from the lemon. (Use the zest only—not the white pith which is bitter). Place in a medium saucepan. Squeeze 1 tsp. fresh juice from the lemon and set aside. Add broth to the saucepan. Cover and simmer over medium heat about 20 minutes. Remove zest.

2) In a second saucepan heat the butter over low heat; when the foam subsides, stir in the flour. Cook, stirring constantly, for two minutes; gradually add warm stock and cream, whisking constantly, until soup is thickened, 3 to 5 minutes. Stir in lemon juice; add garnish and salt and pepper to taste.

Lemon Blueberry Cream Scones

<u>Ingredients</u>

1 1/3 cups cake flour

3 tablespoons sugar

2 tsp. baking powder

1/8 tsp. salt

3 tablespoons unsalted butter

3/4 cup blueberries

1/3 cup heavy cream

1/2 tsp. vanilla

<u>Directions</u>

1) Preheat oven to 425 degrees F. Combine cake flour, sugar, baking powder, and salt in large mixing bowl. Dice butter into small pieces. Use pastry blended to cut into dry ingredients. Gently fold in blueberries.

2) Mix together buttermilk and vanilla; stir into flour mixture. Knead twice. Pat into circle and cut into 8 wedges. Bake for 12-14 minutes.

Lemon Glaze

<u>Ingredients</u>

1/2 cup lemon juice

2 cups confectioners' sugar

1 tablespoon unsalted butter

2 tsp. lemon zest

<u>Directions</u>

Place lemon juice and confectioners' sugar in microwave-safe bowl. Microwave at full power for 30 seconds; whisk in butter and lemon zest, stirring until no lumps remain. Drizzle warm glaze over the top of the scones.

Lemon Meringue Pie

<u>Ingredients for the Crust</u>
1 cup flour
1/2 tsp. salt
4 tablespoons unsalted butter
1/3 cup sour cream
1 tablespoon milk

<u>Directions</u>
1) Preheat oven to 425 degrees F. Place flour, salt, and butter in bowl of food processor. Cut in butter using on/off pulses. Mixture will resemble coarse crumbs. Add sour cream and pulse until blended. Add milk and process until dough forms. Gather dough into a ball.

2) Place a sheet of waxed paper on work surface and flour lightly. Place dough in center of floured waxed paper, turn over to coat both sides with flour. Place a second sheet of waxed paper over top of dough. (You now have a 'sandwich' of waxed paper, floured dough, and waxed paper). Using rolling pin, gently roll dough into an 11-inch circle.

3) Remove top layer of waxed paper and then gently drape back on dough. You are doing this to release the dough so that it no longer adheres to the waxed paper. Quickly flip the dough/waxed paper sandwich over and remove the other sheet of waxed paper.

4) Gently ease the dough into 9-inch pie plate, being careful to not stretch the dough. Crimp the edges as desired. Prick the dough all over with a fork at 1/2-inch intervals. Place aluminum foil over the prepared crust and press it against the dough. Bake for 6 minutes. Remove foil and then bake for another 8-10 minutes or until golden brown. Remove from oven and set aside.

Ingredients for Filling and Meringue
1 1/2 cups water
1 cup sugar
1/2 cup fresh lemon juice
6 large egg yolks (save the whites for the meringue!!)
5 tablespoons cornstarch
2 tsp. grated lemon peel
1/4 tsp. salt
2 tablespoons unsalted butter
5 large egg whites (from the eggs used in the filling—discard one or reserve for another use)
8 tablespoons confectioners' sugar

Directions
1) Whisk together the first 7 ingredients in a heavy medium-sized saucepan to blend. Cook and stir over medium heat until filling thickens and just begins to boil, 8-10 minutes. Remove from heat. Whisk in butter; spoon hot filling into the baked crust.

2) Preheat oven to 300 degrees F. Place egg whites and sugar in stainless steel or heat-safe bowl. Place over pan of simmering water and whisk until eggs are barely warm to the touch—about 2 minutes. Using electric mixer beat egg whites at low speed until foamy. Increase speed to medium-high and continue to beat eggs until stiff glossy peaks form, about 5 minutes. Spread meringue over warm lemon filling, mounding in center and being sure to seal meringue to crust edges. Bake pie for 30 minutes. Reduce oven temperature to 275 degrees F. and continue to bake until meringue is golden brown and set when pie is shaken slightly, 10 to 20 minutes more.

Chicken Picatta

<u>Ingredients</u>
2 boneless, skinless chicken breasts
Salt and fresh ground pepper
1/2 cup flour for dredging
6 tablespoons unsalted butter
4 tablespoons olive oil
1/3 cup fresh lemon juice
1/2 cup chicken broth
2 tablespoons capers, rinsed and drained
1/3 cup fresh parsley, minced

<u>Directions</u>
1) Butterfly each chicken breast and then cut in half to make four thin cutlets. (Not sure what to do? Don't worry; full instructions are given on the next page). Season chicken with salt and pepper. Dredge with flour and shake off excess.

2) Place 2 tablespoons of the butter and 2 tablespoons of the olive oil in a large skillet. Melt over medium-high heat. When butter and oil start to sizzle, add 2 pieces of chicken and cook for 3 minutes. When chicken is browned, flip and cook other side for 3 minutes. Remove and transfer to plate.

3) Melt 2 more tablespoons of butter and the remaining 2 tablespoons of olive oil. When the butter and oil start to sizzle add the other 2 pieces of chicken and brown both sides in the same manner as described above. Remove your pan from the heat and place the chicken on the plate.

4) In the same pan add the lemon juice, broth, and capers. Return to the stove and bring to a boil over medium-high heat. Scrape up any browned bits from the bottom of the pan. Taste for seasoning.

5) Return all chicken to the pan and simmer for 5 minutes. Remove chicken to a platter. Add the remaining 2 tablespoons of butter to the sauce and whisk vigorously. Pour sauce over chicken and garnish with parsley.

How to butterfly a chicken breast

. Notice that the chicken breast has a flat side, and a side that is more rounded or plump. Place the chicken breast on your cutting board, plump-side up.

.

. Place the palm of your hand on top of the chicken breast to hold it in place. With your other hand horizontally glide a sharp knife through the breast. Don't cut all the way through; stop within about 1/2 inch of the edge. Imagine that the chicken breast is a book. The uncut edge is the spine of the book.

.

. Open the chicken breast (again, thinking of a book). Cover with a sheet of plastic wrap. Pound the chicken breast with a meat mallet, a rolling pin, or the edge of a plate to create an even thickness.

.

. You now have a thin chicken cutlet that will cook quickly and be incredibly tender.

PEARS

"The pear is the grandfather of the apple, its poor relation…which once, in our humid land, lived lonely and lordly, preserving the memory of its prestige by its haughty comportment." **–Francois Pierre de la Varenne** *("Le Cuisinier françois" one of the most influential French cookbooks)*

Based on the above quote, one might assume that Varenne regarded the pear as a "lesser" fruit, once heralded but now fallen into disregard in comparison to the well-known (and appreciated) apple.

Little did he know that 300 years later annual pear production in the world would exceed 23,580,845 metric tons. Underappreciated? I think not. Nevertheless, pears were grown long before that authority on French cuisine wrote his famous book. Historians believe 7,000 years ago, in the foothills of Tian Shan, a Chinese diplomat grew pears. No, it was more than that; he was obsessed with pears. He abandoned his career and begin a business of grafting and selling pear trees. The fruit he produced, Pyrus communis, is said to be the mother of many of the varieties of pear found throughout the world today. From that mountain range in central Asia, the pear fruit of Mr. Feng Li spread north and south.

But at the same time, wild pears were also growing in Europe. In *"The Odyssey"*, Homer called them a "gift of the gods." Traces of pears have been found in prehistoric areas near Lake Zurich. And Pliny wrote of them in his treatise *"Natural History"*.

And then...the story traveled to the New World. In the 1600s colonists brought pear trees, but blight nearly wiped out the entire pear population. Thankfully, pioneers migrating west in the 1800s had far greater success; their pear trees not only survived, but thrived in the rich volcanic soils and climate of the Pacific Northwest. Today most pears grown in the United States are from the states of New York, Pennsylvania, Michigan, California, Oregon, and Washington, with the west coast states as the top three.

I love pears for their versatility. They can be used in every course of your meal, from appetizer, to salad, to main dish, and dessert. I'm sharing two recipes with you—a pear appetizer (which really isn't a recipe at all), and a breakfast treat that could also be an over-the-top dessert.

Pear Crostini with Blue Cheese and Honey

Ingredients
1 baguette
Extra-virgin olive oil
Honey (your favorite flavor)
Roquefort, Gorgonzola, or Stilton blue cheese
One pear, cored and thinly sliced (Bosc or Asian are wonderful in this dish because of they tend to be more crisp)

Directions
1) Preheat oven to 350 degrees F. Slice the baguette on the diagonal into 1/2-inch thick slices. Brush both sides of the bread with olive oil and then arrange on a rimmed baking sheet. Bake 5 minutes, turn, and bake 5 minutes more or until golden and crisp on the edges. Remove from oven.

2) While still hot, top toasted bread with cheese, then a slice of pear. Drizzle with honey. Serve warm.

French Toast with Caramelized Pears and Brie

<u>Ingredients for the Pear Topping</u>
2 medium Bosc pears
1/4 cup brown sugar
1 tsp. ground cinnamon
1 tablespoon butter, softened

<u>Directions</u>
Pare and thinly slice pears. Place in mixing bowl; sprinkle with sugar and cinnamon. Stir gently to coat and let sit for 30 minutes. Heat butter in large sauté pan over medium heat. Add pears with their juices and cook and stir until fruit softens and juices become syrupy.

<u>Ingredients for the French Toast</u>
1 baguette
3 ounces brie, chilled
1 1/2 cups of milk
2 large eggs
Pinch of salt
1 tablespoon butter, divided

<u>Directions</u>
1) Slice the baguette on the diagonal, making the slices about 1 1/2 inches thick. Discard the ends or save for another use. With a sharp knife, cut a slit in the bottom (crust) side of each slice. Cut the chilled brie into small wedges, about 1/4-inch thick and 1-inch square. Stuff one wedge of brie into each slice of baguette.

2) In a shallow bowl beat together the milk, eggs, and salt with a wire whisk until well blended. Dip the baguette slices into the milk/egg batter, turning to coat both cut sides. Heat a large sauté pan over medium heat. Add 1 tsp. of the butter; as it melts tilt the pan to coat the bottom. Add as many of the baguette slices as will fit in the pan without crowding. Cook until golden on one side (about 2 minutes). Flip and cook other side until brown. Remove from pan and keep warm. Repeat with remaining butter and baguette slices. Top with warm pears.

TOMATOES

"A world without tomatoes is like a string quartet without violins." – **Laurie Colwin**

From where did the idea originate that the forbidden fruit in the Garden of Eden was an apple? Let's review the story. We are told in Genesis that Adam and Eve were living the perfect life in Eden. They could eat fruit from any tree except one, 'the tree of the knowledge of good and evil." Guess what? They ate the forbidden fruit and were expelled from Paradise. The original Hebrew says only "fruit," but in latter-day Western art, ranging from serious religious painting to about a million cartoons, the fruit of temptation is invariably depicted as an apple. I don't think so. My vote is that it was a tomato.

Think about it. On a summer day is there anything more fragrant, sweet, or (dare I say) Heavenly than a plump ripe tomato, warmed by the sun? If you have grown your own tomatoes, or are fortunate enough to be the BFF of someone else who does, I'm sure you'll agree with me.

However, if the tomato did not originate in Garden of Eden…where? Historians believe that the Aztecs were cultivating the tomato plant as early as 700 A.D. Cortez conquered the Aztec city of Tenochtitlan (now named Mexico City) in 1521, and it's assumed that he and his explorers carried tomato seeds back to Europe. (By the way—did you know that tomato is 'tomatl" in the language of the Aztec?)

One hundred years after Cortez transported those seeds to Europe, Tournefort, a French botanist, gave tomato the botanical name *Lycopersicon esculentum*. Loosely translated this means "wolfpeach"—peach because it is round, and wolf because it was thought to be poisonous. If the tomato didn't lead Adam and Eve to commit the original sin, why then did it have such a bad reputation? (Clearly, the poor, lowly tomato needed a public relations manager.) Here's the answer: In the 16th century, aristocrats who dined on tomatoes were falling ill and dying. As a result the tomato was nicknamed "poison apple." However, no one noticed that peasants who ate tomatoes were not affected. So what was the problem? Wealthy Europeans ate on pewter plates, which have a high lead content. The high acid level of tomatoes leached lead from the plates, so the prosperous were perishing from lead poisoning!

Tomatoes traveled back across the Atlantic with American colonists in the 17th century but were used more as an ornamental plant (and named the Love Apple) rather than as a source of food. Since the tomato is a member of the Solanaceae family (which includes deadly nightshade), it was once again looked upon with skepticism and painted with guilt by association.

But the American Civil War changed the life of the lowly tomato. They were known to grow quickly and hold up well under the canning process, so canned tomatoes were fed to the Union army. Guess what? The troops didn't die (at least from eating canned tomatoes). As a result, post-war demand for canned products (including tomatoes) grew. This meant that more farmers were needed. And the rest, as they say, is history. Well, almost. The only tomatoes that were common at the time were the small cherry- and pear-shaped ones. Larger tomatoes were ugly, lumpy, and misshapen. This too changed when a gentleman named Alexander Livingston became interested in the tomato plant. The first one he ever saw was growing wild, and his mother cautioned him not to touch it. "Even the hogs will not eat them" she is reported to have said. In his book *"**Livingston and the Tomato**"*, he wrote:

"There was not in the United States at the time an acre of tomatoes from which a bushel of uniformly smooth tomatoes could be gathered."

After much trial and error Livingston was able to successfully develop a hybrid, which he named the Paragon. He claimed that the 1870 release of the Paragon caused tomato production to

"…increase phenomenally, and rival the potato as a crop to grow…With these, tomato culture began at once to be one of the great enterprises of the country."

I gave up growing my own "forbidden fruits" two decades ago when I moved to deer country. But I can still find just-picked tomatoes at my weekly Farmers Market and at my local produce stand which is open year-round. So, what do you do with fresh tomatoes? Of course you can chop and toss them into a fresh green salad, cut a thick slice and place atop a juicy burger hot off the grill, or simply eat them just as they are. But, if you want to do something more I have a few suggestions. This first recipe was published by Sunset Magazine.

Warm Cioppini Salad

<u>Ingredients</u>
1/2 lb. extra large shrimp, shelled and deveined
3 tablespoons olive oil
2 cups 1/4-inch thick sliced mushrooms
2 cups 1/4-inch thick sliced zucchini
2 cups coarsely chopped fresh tomato
1 1/2 cups drained pitted black ripe olives
Dressing (recipe follows)
3 quarts lightly packed, and crisped fresh spinach leaves
1/2 pound cooked crab

<u>Directions</u>
In a 12-inch skillet over medium heat stir shrimp in oil until pink, about 2 minutes. Lift out and set aside. Add mushrooms and zucchini to pan; stir often on medium-high heat until zucchini is tender-crisp to bite, about 3 minutes. Return shrimp to pan; add tomatoes, olives, and dressing; stir often until hot. Put spinach in wide bowl; pour hot mixture over greens, top with crab, and mix gently.

Dressing:

Mix 1/4 cup lemon juice, 1 tablespoon Worcestershire, and 1 tsp. each dried basil and oregano and minced garlic.

My younger daughter gave me the inspiration for this next recipe; with an over-abundance of tomatoes from her garden she crafted a tomato tart. Great flavors, but the juices of the tomatoes made for a soggy crust. Slow-baking the tomatoes draws out the excess tomato water, concentrates the flavor, and gives you the perfect filling for a cheese-and-tomato filled flaky crust.

Slow-Roasted Tomato Tart

<u>Ingredients</u>
2 pounds Roma or medium-size beefsteak tomatoes
1/4 cup olive oil plus 2 tablespoons olive oil
Salt and freshly-ground black pepper
Fresh thyme sprigs
1 cup plus 2 tablespoons flour
2 tablespoons cold water
Pinch of sea salt
1/2 cup shortening
1 large onion, minced
2 cups grated Cheddar or Swiss cheese
2 tablespoons sour cream

<u>Directions for Tomatoes</u>
1) Preheat oven to 225 degrees F.

2) Cut tomatoes in half lengthwise. Place cut-side up on a rimmed baking sheet. Drizzle with olive oil and season with salt and pepper. Scatter thyme on top. Bake until tomatoes are no longer exuding juice, but still feel plump (this will take anywhere from 4 to 6 hours, depending on the size of your tomatoes).

3) In a small bowl combine the 2 tablespoons of flour and the water; mix with a spoon until smooth. Set aside.

4) In another (medium-sized) bowl combine the remaining 1 cup flour and salt. Cut in the shortening until the mixture resembles coarse crumbs. Add the reserved flour/water mixture. Stir until it forms a ball. Press the dough onto the bottom and up the sides of an ungreased 9-inch pie pan.

<u>How to Finish the Tomato Tart</u>
1) Preheat oven to 375 degrees F.

2) Place onion and olive oil in medium-sized sauté pan; cook over medium heat about 10 minutes or until onion is softened and is beginning to get golden in color. Set aside to cool.

3) Place one half of the cheese in the pastry-lined pan. Stir the sour cream into the cooled sautéed onions. Dollop spoonful's of this mixture evenly over the cheese. Top with the roasted tomatoes, and then the remaining cheese.

4) Bake the tart for 35-40 minutes or until the crust is golden brown. Remove from the oven and let rest at least 10 minutes before serving.

THE SAGA OF HERBS AND SPICES

BASIL

"Tales of toxins and tonics. Sagas of Saviors and scorpions. How did such a beautifully simple (or simply beautiful) plant obtain such a complicated past? Which story are we to believe?" —**Author**

There are those who say that basil tastes of licorice and cloves—a little sweet and a little spicy. My interpretation is far less poetic. For me, basil tastes amazingly, wonderfully, brilliantly…like basil. There is simply no other herb that possesses such heavenly flavor and scent. Please indulge me for just a moment and imagine these three scenarios. A sun-warmed fresh tomato is cut into thick slices and layered with freshly made mozzarella cheese and the top-most leaves of a basil plant, snipped just moments ago. Perhaps you would enjoy homemade pasta tossed with a fruity virgin olive oil, a grinding of fresh black pepper, shavings of Pecorino-Romano cheese, and a chiffonade of basil leaves. Or do you prefer thick slices of crusty ciabatta bread, brushed with olive oil and grilled until gently golden, the edges slightly charred. A spoonful (or more) of garlicky pesto is placed on top. The warmth of the bread melts the stunning green sauce and every crevice of the bread is filled with the flavor and fragrance of basil oil.

It might seem that basil plays little more than a supporting role in many dishes. But is there a Mediterranean cook who could do without it? I believe in every Tuscan kitchen sits a wooden dowel for rolling pasta, a deep kettle for simmering Bolognese, and a mortar and pestle stained green from years of pounding basil leaves. Since basil is held in such great esteem in the Mediterranean one might assume that to be its birthplace. Not so. The history of basil spans at least 5,000 years and begins on another continent.

Some historians believe that basil originated in Africa. Egyptians used it for embalming more than 4,000 years ago. And the Ebers Papyrus (c. 1,550 B.C.) mentions it in a list of 700 herbal medicines. But other researchers theorize that basil originated in India. Tulsi (holy basil) is indigenous to the lower hills of Punjab and the area south of Pakistan. This lush area is blessed with a perfect climate—mild springs and warm summer rainy seasons—just right for growing basil. The people of India cherish tulsi for its healing properties; and for those of the Hindu faith, tulsi is an essential part of the worship of Vishnu.

So it was vital to Egyptians and revered in India, but when basil left home it fell into bad repute. In the year 350 B.C. Alexander the Great brought basil to Greece, and there began her decline from glory. Ancient Greeks associated basil with misfortune; they believed it would flourish only in areas where there was poverty, hatred, and abuse. Greeks came to believe that basil could only successfully be sown if the seeds were cast while ranting and swearing. In fact, the French verb *semer le baslic* (sowing basil) means 'to rant."

Four hundred years later, the situation for basil improved ever so slightly. In the 1st century A.D. it was thought that basil was the only cure for the bite of the basilisk—a mythical dragon-like creature appearing as part snake, part bat, and part rooster. Basil's effectiveness against the basilisk thus imbued it with the magical ability to cure insect stings and animal bites. But strangely enough, herbalists at the same time were theorizing that basil leaves left unattended would turn into a scorpion, and that simply smelling basil would cause a scorpion to form in ones brain. Poor basil—love is fleeting.

In the early 4th century the legend of basil took an entirely different turn. St. Helena, the mother of Emperor Constantine, was credited with discovering relics of the original cross on which Jesus Christ was crucified. According to legend, Helena was led to the site by following a trail of basil—basil which purportedly sprang from the places where Jesus' blood was shed and fell to the ground.

Basil was introduced to Northern Europe in 1,500 A.D. (give or take a few years) where it once again well into disrepute. The English held it in contempt because it would not grow when planted next to rue (a plant thought to provide protection against poisons; therefore anything that would not flourish next to it was held in suspicion.)

Though favored today as a culinary herb, there are still fables and tales attached to basil. In Crete, basil is considered an emblem of Satan and is placed on window ledges to repel him. But in Romania, if a boy accepts a sprig of basil from a girl, they are engaged to be married. I don't know about warding off the devil, but I think basil is Heavenly. Does it attract a soul mate? My husband and I have been married for over 35 years and I use basil in many of our meals. I doubt that basil is the only key to our successful marriage, but I'll keep cooking with it. Why take chances?

Bread salad is a common (and thrifty) meal in northern Italy which is where I first tasted it. Why toss out perfectly good (though slightly stale) bread, when you can toss it with a few fresh ingredients and make this wonderful dish?

Bread Salad (Panzanella)

Ingredients for 2 Servings
4-5 slices day old rustic bread
1 cucumber, peeled and chopped
4 small Roma tomatoes, or 1-2 large beefsteak, heirloom, or tomato of your choice
1/4 of a red onion, thinly sliced
5-10 basil leaves sliced into thin ribbons (chiffonade)
3 tablespoons olive oil
1 tablespoon vinegar
Salt and pepper to taste

Directions
1) Take the day-old bread, and lightly moisten under running water. The bread should be moistened all the way through. If it's too wet, gently squeeze excess water from the bread with your hands and set aside while chopping vegetables. The bread should crumble, not clump/collapse or get soggy.

2) Shred the bread into a large salad bowl. I like to keep some larger pieces of bread in my panzanella, but you can crumble the bread down until there are very fine pieces, or "breadcrumbs" that resemble couscous.

3) Dice the tomatoes and add to the bowl along with the cucumbers and onion. Add vinegar and olive oil and mix completely.

Other Suggested Add-ins

. roasted bell pepper, diced
. diced zucchini
. diced yellow summer squash
. fresh steamed asparagus tips
. crisp broccoli florets

. drained garbanzo beans (chickpeas)

. crumbled feta cheese
. shaved pecorino Romano cheese
. crumbled blue cheese

. crisp crumbled bacon
. chopped walnuts
. hard-cooked eggs, chopped

BLACK PEPPER

"The disparity between a restaurant's price and food quality rises in direct proportion to the size of the pepper mill." – **Bryan Q. Miller** *(American television and comic writer)*

"Would you like some freshly ground pepper with that?"

Every day thousands of waitpersons in thousands of restaurants ask that question. Peppermills near the size of the Seattle Space Needle hover expectantly over dinner plates, soups, and salads, anxious to adorn our "almost perfect meal" with a light shower of flavorful black dots. Today this daily ritual of pepper presentation is routine, perfunctory, and inexpensive. No seasoning, other than salt, is more common. But this wasn't always the case.

The pepper vine (*Piper nigrum*), native to Kerala, a province in southwest India, has been prized since ancient times and was once one of the most valuable substances on earth. Not only could its sharpness enliven otherwise bland foods, it could disguise the flavor of foods that were, let's say, somewhat less than fresh (a big consideration in times when refrigeration did not exist). However, black pepper was far more than a seasoning. It was used as a currency (along with gold) to pay tolls, taxes, and ransoms and was a sacred offering to the Greek gods. The quest to discover new paths to these "riches of the Orient" led to exploration by Portuguese sailors and the Spanish monarchy. It was due to these travels that many new lands were discovered and major merchant cities were established in Europe and the Middle East. Black pepper is still, by monetary value, the most widely traded spice in the world, accounting for 20 percent of all spice imports.

The ingredients in this recipe are so every day, so commonplace, you might assume that the dish is dull and commonplace as well. It is said that Roman soldiers carried dry pasta, hard-aged cheese and black pepper (ingredients that would not spoil) with them so that they could make this dish while "on the road". If it carried the Roman army, I think it's worth a try.

Pasta with Pepper and Pecorino Romano Cheese (*Cacio e pepe*)

Ingredients (for 2 servings)
1/2 pound spaghetti or other dried pasta of your choice
1 cup grated Grana Padano cheese
2 tsp. coarsely ground black pepper
3/4 cup Pecorino Romano cheese, finely shredded
Juice of one lemon
Good quality olive oil

Directions
Bring a large pot of salted water to a boil over high heat. Add pasta and cook according to package directions until al dente. Drain the pasta, reserving 1 cup of the cooking water. While the pasta is cooking combine the Grana Padano and black pepper in a large serving bowl. Remove about 1/4 cup of the pasta water with a ladle and stir into the Grana Padano/black pepper mixture. Whisk briskly to combine and create the sauce. When the pasta is cooked, drain well and pour into the bowl. Toss; add the Pecorino Romano and lemon juice; toss again. Serve immediately with a drizzle of olive oil on each serving.

A Timeline of the Pepper Trade

1000 B.C. – Arabian traders enjoyed a huge monopoly in the spice business. To protect their valuable routes, they created stories of dragons guarding the pepper groves.

40 A.D. – The Romans had a thriving trade in pepper, carried by July monsoon winds from the southwestern coast of India to Alexandria. (Apparently they were not afraid of dragons).

476 A.D. – With the fall of the Roman Empire, other groups began to take over the spice trade. Under the unifying influence of Islam, Arabs once again organized and became dominant in the trade of pepper.

10th Century A.D. – By this time pepper had become important in Europe. It is reported that English King Ethelred II (978-1016) required 10 pounds of pepper from German spice traders as payment for doing business in London.

15th Century A.D. – By the end of this century spice merchants from Alexandria were bringing pepper to Venice, over 400 tons every year. Thus Venice became the distribution center for pepper in Europe, and they marked up the price about 40 percent! This Venetian price-gouging was enough to spur the rest of Europe into exploration. And so began the age of Christopher Columbus, Vasco de Gama, Sir Francis Drake and other explorers.

1500 to 1600 A.D. – de Gama was the first person to reach India by sailing around Africa. The Portuguese controlled the spice trade, importing about 2 million kilograms of pepper each year. But this dominance came at a considerable price. It is estimated that up to 30 percent of Portuguese trading vessels were lost enroute.

17th Century – The Dutch established colonies in Bantam, Ceylon, Java, Lompong, and Malabar and thus became dominant players in the spice trade.

CLOVES

"The quest for cloves is one of those events that shaped world history; it spawned expeditions, created monopolies, generated fantastic wealth, and brought about great suffering". –**Author**

Baked ham. Pumpkin pie. Mulled wine. Warm, indulgent, comfort foods. What unites them all? Obviously, we enjoy them during the Christmas holidays. And…they all contain cloves—that super-strong, hot-sweet spice.

The use of cloves seems to reach a frenzied peak during the holidays, but why? Perhaps this phenomenon traces back to long ago in Europe when all spices were scarce—and expensive. Back then, cloves were a sign of indulgence, a show of wealth or a rare prize, and were reserved for special occasions, like Christmas. Indeed, cloves provide a flavor boost to rich, hearty winter foods, so it's no wonder that it has become the "Christmas spice." Cloves has a warm, bold aroma and a sharp, almost hot flavor which is tempered by cooking.

Like many spices, the history of cloves spans centuries. It is thought that the Chinese were the first to discover the Indonesian islands called the *Moluccas*. They returned home with cloves, which were used in pharmaceuticals, and as a breath freshener. (Legend tells that one was required to chew cloves prior to having audience with the Emperor, lest he be offended with bad breath.)

Arab traders were next to find the Moluccas, and centuries later the ships of Magellan embarked on a trip around the world, finding the Moluccas enroute. Magellan's fleet returned to Spain in 1522 A.D., loaded with cloves and nutmeg; the value of the cargo supporting the cost of the voyage many times over. Cloves were in high demand in Europe to preserve meat, and gross profit margins for those who bought it could reach as much as 2,000%. (Once could say that money really **does** grow on trees.) This made the cloves trade worth fighting over, and several European nations did just that.

The Portuguese established the first monopoly, but were pushed out in 1605 by Dutch explorers who had discovered their own route to the Molucca Islands. In their zeal to control the clove industry, lords of the Dutch East India Company destroyed clove trees growing anywhere outside of their jurisdiction; with that act the suffering began. Natives of the Moluccas had a spiritual connection with the clove trees; it was part of their tradition to plant one tree for each child born. The fate of the child was then linked to the life (and death) of the tree. Destruction of those trees was the ultimate crime, and in 1816 the natives revolted in a bloody battle.

One might say that Divine providence stepped in. We now know that decades earlier a French missionary had managed to smuggle clove seeds to Zanzibar and Mauritius. With that, world production of clove spice rose—and with the rule of economics, that increase in supply caused prices to plummet. Eventually the cost of wars, blockades, and battles became too costly; the 200-year monopoly of the clove spice trade ended in bankruptcy for the East India Company.

The pumpkin scones on the next page bring together many of the flavors and ingredients common to the Molucca Islands. Pumpkin is customarily used to make steamed cakes and other sweets; brown sugar and coconut milk are staples in an Indonesian pantry, and cloves and nutmeg are the spices that were so fervently desired by explorers.

Pumpkin Spice Scones

Ingredients for Scones
2 cups flour
1/3 cup brown sugar
1 tablespoon baking powder
1/2 tsp. salt
1 tsp. cinnamon
1/2 tsp. nutmeg
1/4 tsp. ground cloves
1/4 tsp. ginger
6 tablespoons butter, cut into small pieces
1/2 cup pumpkin puree (not canned pumpkin pie filling)
3 tablespoons coconut milk (or whole milk)
1 egg
1 cup plus 3 tablespoons powdered sugar
2 tablespoons milk
1/4 tsp. cinnamon
1 pinch each of nutmeg, ginger, and cloves

Directions
1) Preheat oven to 425 degrees F.

2) Line a baking sheet with parchment paper. In large mixing bowl whisk together flour, sugar, baking powder, salt, cinnamon, nutmeg, cloves, and ginger. Using a pastry blender, cut in the butter until the mixture resembles coarse crumbs.

3) In a separate bowl, mix together the pumpkin, milk, and egg. Add the pumpkin mixture to the dry ingredients. Mix until just combined. Pat the dough out on a lightly floured surface to form a rectangle that is roughly 4 inches by 12 inches. Cut the dough into thirds to form three 4 inch by 4 inch squares, then cut an X in each of the squares to form 4 triangular scones.

5) Move the scones to the prepared baking sheet and bake 14-16 minutes, or until lightly browned on the bottom. Remove from the oven and let cool. While the scones are cooling, make the spiced glaze. Whisk together the powdered sugar, milk, and spices; drizzle the spiced glaze over the scones.

GINGER

"Had I but a penny in the world, thou shouldst have it for gingerbread." –**William Shakespeare**

Merchants and Monarchs, Sages and Sheep—The story of this beautiful fragrant flowering plant begins as do many of our tales about treasured herbs and spices—deep within the heart of India. It is there that anthropologists have found remnants, tiny fragments of ginger root used 5,000 years ago; in the beginning, long before the written word, long before Man began to record his own history.

"Do not eat too much. Do not talk during meals. Do not take away the ginger." –*Confucius*

We know that ginger also grew in China; **wise men** in traditional Chinese and Ayurvedic Indian systems viewed it as a healing gift from God. From its origin to the present, ginger has been the world's most widely cultivated herb. Historians believe that by the 5th century, ginger was being transported in trade ships to what was then the far reaches of the Earth—Rome—where it was used both as a medicine and a flavoring agent. Ginger was a highly valued trade commodity. However, with the decline of the Roman Empire, this precious (and costly) herb almost fell from existence in Europe. Arab merchants stepped in and began to control the export of ginger from India; in addition they developed a new market in Africa where ginger proved to be a treatment for malaria and yellow fever.

Today ginger can be found in any grocery store, and for just a few dollars, but in the 13th century it was so highly valued that **one pound cost the same as a whole live sheep.**

Thusfar I've written of the merchants, the sages, and the sheep. Who is the monarch in this tale? By medieval times ginger was being preserved and imported to England for use in sweets. A common use was "gingerbread" and none other than **Queen Elizabeth I of England** originated the idea of forming gingerbread into the likeness of visiting dignitaries.

Ginger can be used in so many ways. While it is still relevant as a tonic, ginger is an aromatic, pungent, and spicy herb that lends a special flavor and zest to so many dishes—desserts, beverages, stir fries, and even main dishes like these ginger prawns.

Orange Ginger Prawns

<u>Ingredients</u>
1 1/2 cups orange juice
2 tablespoons honey
2 tablespoons orange marmalade
2 tsp. fresh ginger root, grated
2 tsp. low-sodium soy sauce
1/4 tsp. lime juice
2 pounds large shrimp peeled and deveined, (about 1/2 pound per person)
Bamboo skewers (soaked in warm water for 30 minutes)

<u>Directions</u>
1) Pour orange juice into a small saucepan. Bring to a simmer over medium-high heat; cook until reduced to 1/2 cup (about 8 minutes). Set aside to cool slightly.

2) Remove saucepan from heat. Stir in marmalade, fresh ginger root, soy sauce, and lime juice. Set aside.

3) Thread 4 or 5 (depending on size) shrimp on each bamboo skewer, piercing each near the head and the tail. Don't crowd them together too closely—you want them to cook evenly.

4) Preheat grill to medium, or about 325 to 350 degrees. (The grill is medium hot if you can hold your hand about 4 inches above the coals for only 6 to 8 seconds).Oil the grill lightly; place the skewered shrimp directly on the grill over medium heat.

5) Grill for 2 to 3 minutes on one side and then turn. Brush with orange sauce; continue grilling 1 to 2 more minutes until they turn pink, then remove from heat immediately. Do not overcook the shrimp or they will become tough and rubbery. Brush shrimp once again with sauce. Serve additional sauce on the side.

This compilation of stories and recipes would not be complete without mention of my sister Florence. Of six surviving children I was number 6 (the youngest) and she was the oldest, 26 years my senior. During the work week she was the one who cleaned the house, did the laundry, tended the garden, and prepared our evening meal. Our Mom was the master of pasta, pastries, pies and homemade breads, but it was Florence who was the doyen of cakes, frosting and mouth-watering cookies, and these were my favorite:

Florence's Slice and Bake Spice Cookies

Ingredients
1/2 cup butter
1/2 cup shortening
1/2 cup sugar
1/2 cup brown sugar
1 egg
2 tablespoons milk
1/2 tsp. vanilla
2 1/4 cups flour
1/2 tsp. baking soda
1/2 tsp. salt
1/4 tsp. nutmeg
1/4 tsp. ginger

Directions
1) Place butter in large mixing bowl; beat at medium speed with electric mixer for 30 seconds. Add sugars and beat until light and fluffy.

2) Add egg, milk, and vanilla; beat until well blended. Add flour and spices and beat again until well blended. Stir in nuts. Shape into two 7-inch long rolls. Wrap in wax paper and chill at least 6 hours.

3) Preheat oven to 375 degrees F. Cut dough into 1/4-inch thick slices. Place 1-inch apart on lightly greased cooking sheets. Bake 8-10 minutes or until golden. Let sit on cookie sheet 1 minute before moving to cooling rack.

NUTMEG

"Nutmeg has been one of the saddest stories in history." –**Michael Krondl**, *Culinary Historian*

East of Java is an archipelago of ten tiny islands, beautiful volcanic rocks surrounded by white beach sands and a deep ocean abyss. Warm, crystal-clear waters and colorful reefs teem with marine life; they beckon divers to explore this place, one of the most unspoiled dive spots on the planet. These are the Banda Islands…and they are covered with nutmeg trees.

In an analysis of position, it seems that the size of this idyllic island chain was inversely proportionate to its impact on history. Ancient writings don't disclose who first discovered the riches hanging in the fragrant Myristica trees. But we do know that before the 6th century A.D. nutmeg had been carried to Byzantium—a Greek colony which was later named Constantinople, and later still, Istanbul. Arab traders bartered the spice as far west as Rome where it was used not just as a flavoring, but was prized even more for its powers as a tonic and aphrodisiac.

Nutmeg was always fantastically expensive—a 14th century German price table lists the value of a pound of the spice as equivalent to 'seven fat oxen." (One might think of it as the Beluga caviar of the 1300's.) In 1453 the Ottoman Turks conquered Constantinople; their embargo of this western route forced Europeans to seek a new eastern trade route.

Columbus sailed the Atlantic looking for just such a passage, and in 1497 Vasco da Gama rounded the Cape of Good Hope and landed on the Malabar Coast (India) proclaiming it "For Christ and spices!" He was close, but still so far away. Eventually it was the Portuguese in 1511 who annexed the Molucca islands of Indonesia, of which Banda is a small part. The fortresses established there sealed the deal on a monopoly which would last almost 100 years.

In the 1600's the Dutch East India Company (*Vereenigde Oost-Indische Compagnie or VOC*) seized all but one of the Banda Islands and enslaved the native populace. The death penalty was imposed on any soul suspecting of selling nutmeg outside of the VOC. When a few islanders dared ignore the threat, the company president, Jan Pieterszoon Coen, ordered the beheading of every Banda male over the age of 15. Within 15 years the original population of 15,000 was reduced to 600.

But there was still Run Island. That's the one island of the ten that was not under the thumb of the Netherlands. The English controlled it, and for the next 60 years there were countless skirmishes and truces between England and the Netherlands. Eventually a compromise was reached. The English agreed to swap Run Island for a small trading post in the Americas. Perhaps you have heard of it?—Manhattan.

By 1669 VOC was employing 50,000 people, utilizing 10,000 soldiers and 200 ships, and still was able to pay its shareholders an annual dividend of 40 percent. This perfect, absolute control began to fall apart however when Pierre Poivre, a French horticulturalist (perhaps the Johnny Appleseed of nutmeg?), smuggled out nutmeg seeds and successfully transplanted trees in the French colonies of Mauritius.

Why was nutmeg spice so highly coveted? One factor was simply the economic principle of supply and demand—nutmeg was very rare. And it was purported to have the ability to ward off the plague—a handy thing to have on hand during the Black Death. Who knows—fleas seem to dislike the smell of nutmeg, so perhaps there really **is** something to the "medicine" of nutmeg.

I doubt you can find another spice with such a lofty reputation; not only was nutmeg heralded as a preventative of the plague, it was also credited with the ability to reduce the signs of aging, cure impotence, lower cholesterol, reduce anxiety, AND act as a (questionably effective) narcotic. However, one would have to ingest a Herculean quantity—2 ounces—of the stuff—to obtain a high. (Keep in mind that an entire cheesecake will probably contain no more than 1/2 tsp). And no other spice has the intense, sweet but musky flavor of nutmeg. Blame it on **myristicin**—a volatile oil found in other plants (carrots, celery, dill, and parsley) but in over-the-top quantities in nutmeg.

You've probably tasted nutmeg in cakes and cookies, chai tea, or perhaps sprinkled atop a warm cup of eggnog. But if that is your only use of nutmeg you're missing out indeed. The earthy taste of nutmeg marries perfectly with creamy/savory foods as well.. Add a pinch to your next squash bisque, a dash in your Alfredo sauce, or a dab in any dish with Swiss or Gruyere cheese. Italian grandmothers add a skosh to their potato gnocchi. You might even put some in your seafood chowder.

Scallop Chowder

<u>Ingredients</u>
1 large onion, minced
2 stalks celery, diced
2 **tsp.** olive oil
6 slices bacon, diced
1 pound bay scallops
4 tablespoons butter
4 tablespoons flour
3/4 cup dry white wine
1 14-oz can chicken broth
2 large russet potatoes
1 1/2 cups half and half
Salt and pepper, to taste
1/4 tsp. ground nutmeg
1 tablespoon dry cooking sherry
Parsley to garnish

<u>Directions</u>
1) Place onions, celery, and olive oil in large stock pot over medium-high heat. Cook about 2 minutes, or until vegetables begin to soften. Add bacon and continue to cook, stirring constantly, until bacon begins to brown and becomes crisp. Remove bacon and vegetables from pot and set aside.

2) Place one-half of scallops in stock pot and cook without stirring for one minute. Stir gently to loosen scallops from bottom of pan and cook 30 seconds more. Remove from pan. Repeat this process with the remainder of the scallops. Remove scallops from the pot and set aside.

3) Add butter to pan; when melted stir in flour; whisk constantly. Peel and finely dice potatoes. Add white wine and potatoes to the pot and simmer until the wine is almost evaporated. Stir in broth and simmer until potatoes are very tender. Stir in half and half; simmer until heated through. Return scallops to pan. Stir in ground nutmeg. Just before serving, stir in cooking sherry. Garnish with parsley and an additional sprinkle of nutmeg.

Nutmeg also provides a subtle but important pop of flavor in egg and cheese dishes, such as Joe's Special. "Joe" and I were introduced to each other years ago when I attended a Christmas Brunch with my office coworkers.

My adventurous side appears when I dine out. I say "why eat something at a restaurant that you cook at home? Live a little." (However, I'm not Anthony Bourdain or Andrew Zimmern crazy). I saw on the menu "Joe's Special"—scrambled eggs with spinach, mushrooms, garlic, onions, and ground beef. Each of those sounds wonderful on their own. Could they taste great together? I was willing to explore—and I'm so glad that I did!

There are many versions of this dish, and it seems that anyone named Joe (or Joseppi) is willing to claim this creation as his own. Some say it was invented to feed hungry California Gold Rush miners. Others say the recipe was created at Joe's Restaurant in the 1930's. The Bunny Bennington band had come in near closing time, and "Joe" whipped up this dish for them with ingredients he had on hand. Who knows? What is certain is that this genius concoction originated in the San Francisco area.

Joe's Special

<u>Ingredients</u>
2 tsp. olive oil
12 ounces ground turkey (7 percent fat)
2 onions, finely chopped
2 cloves garlic, minced
1/2 pound sliced mushrooms
2 cups of fresh spinach, coarsely chopped
4 beaten eggs
1 tsp. dried oregano leaves
1/4 tsp. ground nutmeg
1 tsp. salt
1/4 tsp. pepper
4 tablespoons Parmesan cheese

<u>Directions</u>

1) Heat the olive oil in a large sauté pan over medium-high heat.

2) Add the ground turkey, chopped onions, and minced garlic. Cook until the turkey is almost browned and the onions and garlic are tender.

3) Add the sliced mushrooms and cook until they are soft. Stir in spinach and seasonings (oregano, nutmeg, salt, pepper). Cook the mixture until just heated through.

4) Add the beaten eggs and cook, stirring, until the eggs are firm but still tender. Remove from the heat and stir in the Parmesan cheese.

ROSEMARY

"I'm glad I wore my hiking boots!" —Author

The path from Corniglia to Vernazza is narrow and precarious. To my left is a steep hillside of boulders and stacked rock; on my right are jagged rocks hugging the rugged coastline. Nothing but a fragile railing separates hikers from that dangerous cliff edge…and a plummet of 700 feet to the Ligurian Sea. My husband and I are walking the sinuous cliffside path of The Cinque Terra.

Cinque Terre (Five Lands) is five small coastal villages on the west coast of Italy. Monterosso is the northernmost town; its beach, boardwalk and luxury hotels have earned it the nickname "Italian Riviera".

Next is Vernazza. She holds onto her old-world charm with a quiet harbor under the shadows of an ancient castle. The hills of Vernazza are dotted with ageless olive trees and wine-producing grape vines still tended by hand on steeply terraced slopes. Most of all, Vernaza is about putting aside the frantic pace, inhaling deeply, and taking life at a slower pace.

Unlike her sister villages, Corniglia does not overlook the sea. Brightly-colored four-story houses outline the narrow streets and alleys, and are little changed from the scene described by Boccaccio in his "Decameron" a 1353 A.D. compendium of 100 tales shared by ten travelers who banded together to escape plague-ridden Florence.

Manarolo is the oldest, and second smallest of the five villages. Her primary industries are fishing and wine-making.

Then there is Riomaggiore, a fishing village originally settled by Greek immigrants in the 8th century A.D. Terraced hillsides dotted with grape vines and slate-roofed houses speak of the Greek influence. In the early 20th century a railway was constructed to link the five towns of the Cinque Terra to one another. To aid the construction workers in moving back and forth along the first segment, a path was excavated. One hundred years later that same path is used today by tourists; it's the easiest part of the trail, with magnificent views of the sea. It is here that romantics leave "locks of love" on the fence overlooking the blue waters below. The locals call this place "Via dell'Amore", the Walk of Love.

But I'm not on the Walk of Love; the walk of **dread** is more like it. Did I mention that I don't like heights? Not knees-quaking petrified, but, given the option of viewing the plains of Kansas or contemplating the precipice that could instantly end my life, I think you know which one I would choose.

When my husband and I began this trek, I was inwardly praying for deliverance, but as we progressed, the path widened... The railing looks much more trustworthy, and there's just **so much beauty** to take in. Like a small child distracted by the lollipop at the doctor's office, I've forgotten my fears. Inches from the railing are clusters of prickly pear cactus. Their flowers have long since faded, and are replaced by fat pink globes. If you grasp them carefully (a kerchief will help) they can be split open to reveal honey-sweet, sticky fruit. A peregrine falcon glides on an air current and then dives into the sea, a sea of unbelievable brilliant blue. And, the plant life! The air is filled with the scent of juniper, camphor-like myrtle, the heady perfume of lavender, and *rosemary*.

Rosemary—the beautiful evergreen bush with pine-scented needle-like leaves is associated with memory; its enduring fragrance probably has a lot to do with that. In ancient times rosemary was woven into headpieces for the bride and the groom and guests wore sprigs of rosemary on their clothing.

"There's rosemary, that's for remembrance. Pray you, love, remember." (**Ophelia** *in Hamlet, Act 4, Scene 5*).

By the 17th century rosemary made the voyage across the sea from Europe to America. At that time it was used primarily as a fragrance for soaps, perfumes, and the occasional comfort tea. However, when French and Italian immigrants began to arrive in the late 19th and early 20th centuries, the culinary magic of rosemary was finally discovered.

Cooks throughout the Mediterranean area have had a centuries-long love affair with this fragrant herb. Rosemary (the Latin name is Rosmarinus which means "dew of the sea") thrives in weed-like fashion on the rocky coast, and it flourishes inland as well. What would a meal of Tuscan lamb be without the flavor of rosemary, or a pork loin without Herbs de Provence? The camphor and pine scent of rosemary is unmistakable. And the pleasure of rosemary is inseparable from the places where it grows and the memories those places create. Oh, and about that trek along the hillside path? As soon as we completed our hike to Vernazza, my husband and I found an open-air café and enjoyed a mid-day snack of rosemary focaccia and a glass of vin santo.

Rosemary Focaccia

<u>Ingredients</u>

1/2 pound seedless red grapes
1/4 cup warm water
1/4 tsp. sugar
1 envelope (about 2 tsp.) active dry yeast
3 cups all-purpose flour
3/4 cup warm water
3 tablespoons olive oil
Cooking spray
2 tablespoons olive oil
2 tablespoons fresh rosemary, chopped
Sea salt, to taste

Directions

1) Preheat oven to 300 degrees F.

2) Place the grapes in a baking dish large enough to hold them in a single layer. Bake in the middle rack of the 30 minutes, or until soft and sticky; cool slightly.

3) In a small bowl, combine 1/4 cup warm water with the sugar and yeast. (The temperature of the water should be warm, not hot. If you have ever tested the heat of the milk in a baby bottle you will know what I am talking about. It should be warm on your wrist.) Let the water/yeast mixture stand in a warm place for about 10 minutes, or until it is bubbly and begins to smell yeasty.

4) In another bowl, combine the flour and salt. Make a well in the flour; add the water/yeast mixture, the remaining 3/4 cup warm water, and 3 tablespoons olive oil. Begin mixing flour and liquid with your hand; mix until you form dough that cleans the sides of the bowl.

5) Place the dough on lightly floured surface and begin to knead with the heel of your hand, turning and folding dough. Knead 5 to 8 minutes, or until dough becomes smooth and elastic. Put dough into a clean bowl and let rise, covered with a kitchen towel in a warm place 1 to 2 hours, until doubled in bulk.

6) Preheat oven to 350 degrees F.

7) Coat the bottom of an 11x7-inch baking pan with cooking spray. Pat the dough into the pan. Brush the surface with 2 tablespoons olive oil. Indent the surface of the dough by pressing all over with your fingertips. Evenly distribute grapes over the surface of the dough; sprinkle rosemary and coarse salt on top.

8) Cover with a clean kitchen towel. Let rise in a warm place for about 45 minutes, or until doubled in bulk. Bake for 30 minutes or until puffy and lightly golden on top.

Rosemary flourishes in the Mediterranean **and** in my backyard. It is one of the few plants that is willing to put up with snow in the winter, lack of water in the summer, AND the marauding families of deer who ravage our landscape on a daily basis. This shortbread is not like anything you have tasted before; it's sweet, buttery, and the rosemary provides a subtle savory/piney note.

Rosemary Shortbread Cookies

Ingredients
2 cups all purpose flour
3/4 tsp. salt
1/2 tsp. baking powder
1 tablespoon fresh rosemary, chopped
1 1/2 sticks (3/4 cup) unsalted butter, softened
2 tablespoons mild honey
1/2 cup confectioners' sugar
Garnish--small rosemary sprigs

Directions
1) Preheat oven to 300 degrees F.

2) In a small bowl whisk together the flour, salt, baking powder, and rosemary. In a separate bowl mix together butter, honey, and confectioners" sugar with an electric mixer at low speed, then add flour mixture; mix until dough resembles coarse meal with some small (roughly pea-size) butter lumps.

3) Gather dough into a ball and transfer to a lightly floured surface. Knead dough until it just comes together, about 8 times. Halve dough and form each half into a 5-inch disk. Roll out 1 disk (keep remaining dough at room temperature) between 2 sheets of parchment into a 9-inch round (trim as necessary).

4) Remove top sheet of parchment and transfer dough on bottom sheet of parchment to a baking sheet. Score dough into 8 wedges by pricking dotted lines with a fork, then mark edges decoratively. Arrange rosemary sprigs (if using) decoratively on top of dough, pressing lightly to help adhere, and sprinkle dough with 1/2 tablespoon granulated sugar.

5) Repeat with 2nd round of dough.

6) Bake shortbread in middle of oven until golden brown, 20 to 25 minutes.

7) Slide shortbread on parchment to a rack and cool 5 minutes. Transfer with a metal spatula to a cutting board and cut along score marks with a large heavy knife.

SAGE

"Why should a man die when sage grows in his garden?" – **University of Salerno** *School of Medicine*

What makes sage so amazing, so magical? There is truly no other ingredient on earth that tastes or smells quite like sage. Take a fresh velvety leaf, crush it between your thumb and forefinger, and then breathe in deeply. The first thing you will notice is a hint of pine, not unlike rosemary. Breath again; there is a hint of citrus. Not a grapefruit citrus, not orange, not lime, or even lemon. It's a quiet, earthier citrus, like lemongrass. But that's not all. There is still another elusive note; what does that scent bring to mind? And then it comes to you—eucalyptus. Sage takes you to the distant corners of the earth and then back home, with one gentle touch.

In the United States, whether the center of your Thanksgiving Day feast is a roast turkey, or you enjoy a mix of traditional and new recipes, you will probably reach for sage when you are preparing the food for your table. But the history of sage extends far beyond this yearly festival, and has nothing to do with roast turkey. Sage wasn't used as a seasoning until the 17th century, but its therapeutic properties have been known for thousands of years. In fact, its botanical name, *Salvia*, is derived from the Latin *salvare*, which means to heal. Throughout the millennia sage has been used in countless concoctions; a potion to increase fertility, cure for snakebites, and a local anesthetic.

The importance of sage caught the attention of Charlemagne who recommended that it be cultivated throughout his kingdom. Sage even played a part in warding off the plague; it was also one of the ingredients in Four Thieves Vinegar—a blend of spices thought to be a cure. In 16th century England, sage tea was a popular beverage until trade with China introduced Asian tea leaves. Then a strange thing happened—sage tea fell out of favor in England, but the Chinese acquired a love for the brew and willingly traded their green tea leaves for sage leaves at a ratio of 4:1. Sage was a common plant in 18th century Colonial gardens and was used for both culinary and medicinal purposes. Early American cooks used the pungent herb in chowders, fish, roast poultry, and (as in England) in cheese-making.

Some people complain that the taste is overpowering—don't blame the messenger; blame the cook. Sage is best when used in moderation. A little bit goes a long way. So, use just a little bit, and create an unforgettable homemade sausage for your family; easy to make, lower in fat and sodium than store-bought, and filled with love.

Turkey Breakfast Sausage Patties

Ingredients
1 cup quick oats
3/4 cup spicy V-8 (or you could use Bloody Mary mix)
1 pound ground turkey (please use 93% fat free—the 99% fat free is too dry)
1 1/2 tsp. ground sage
1 tsp. ground black pepper
3/4 tsp. salt
1/2 tsp. ground ginger
1/4 tsp. dried thyme

Directions
1) Soak oats in juice for 15 minutes in a large bowl. Add remaining ingredients and mix until very well blended. Form mixture into a 12-inch log. Wrap and freeze until firm enough to slice, about 1.5 to 2 hours. (Do NOT freeze solid). Cut into 32 slices (about 3/8 inch thick). Place on cookie sheet and freeze until firm. Remove from cookie sheet and store in zip-lock bag for up to 3 months. To cook, pan fry for 8-10 minutes—no need to thaw.

SALT

And God said, "Let the water under the sky be gathered to one place, and let dry ground appear." And it was so. God called the dry ground "land," and the gathered waters he called 'seas." And God saw that it was good. — Genesis 1:9-10

How did it begin, this wondrous blue marble we call home? Proponents of evolution theory envision a random but nonetheless dynamic progression over millions of years. Those who hold onto Creationism acknowledge a Divine creator and the formation of earth just a few millennia ago. Whatever your belief, it's clear that the salty ocean waters (and thus salt) have long been a part of our existence. As the antediluvian seas retreated they left behind salt—exposed in playas and dry lakes, folded into rocks, sheltered in caverns and coursing through lakes and streams.

Today salt is easy to obtain—it's everywhere—and it's inexpensive. But at one time it was one of the most valuable commodities on earth. Salt is an integral part of our being—so much so that it is one of our five sensory tastes (along with sweet, sour, bitter, and umami). Before our birth we were suspended in our mother's wombs in a saline ocean. For thousands of years salt has been used to disinfect, purify, and embalm. In the preparation of food, salt can preserve meats and act as a tenderizer; when used as brine it sharpens and enhances the rind of aging cheese; salt aids in the pickling of vegetables; and inclusion of salt in yeast dough will greatly improve the crumb of a loaf of bread. Salt is the one flavor that sharpens and brightens all others. Any confectioner will tell you that even *sweet* tastes are enhanced with a pinch of salt.

To taste salt is to taste our history as humans on this earth. The Bible contains thirty references to salt—using it as a metaphor for loyalty, usefulness and permanence. Such was the value of salt in ancient times. In the Middle East the only source of salt was the Dead Sea area—hence, it was valued, it was treasured. But Egyptian writings about salt pre-date even those of the Old Testament. As far back as 6,050 B.C., salt was used by the Egyptians as a religious offering; it was a valuable trade commodity between Phoenicians and their rivals in the Mediterranean, and in ancient Greece salt was deemed so valuable that it was exchanged as payment for slaves, giving rise to the expression "not worth his salt."

Food storage is vital for the preservation of a society. Today we have the conveniences of canning, refrigeration and freeze-drying, but these certainly were not available even 100 years ago. Whether hunted or grown and harvested, food is rarely available when it is needed, unless it is somehow stored. Salt's ability to preserve food became a foundation of successful civilizations. It helped to eliminate the dependence on the seasonal availability of food and it allowed travel over long distances.

Historians believe that the city of Rome might have begun as a salt-trading center; of all the roads that led to Rome, one of the busiest was the Via Salaria, the salt route, over which Roman soldiers marched. Salt rations ('*salarium argentum*') were given to those soldiers—the etymology of our word 'salary." Merchants drove oxcarts full of the precious crystals up the Tiber from the salt pans at Ostia. As peoples transported salt and searched for new sources, roads were formed and new civic centers established. For example, Salzburg is literally the "city of salt."

Today technology allows us to mine salt, but thousands of years ago those underground deposits were unobtainable; salt harvests were located in just a few precious areas. Ships bearing salt from Egypt to Greece traversed the Mediterranean and the Aegean Seas and as early as the 6th century Moorish merchants routinely traded salt, ounce for ounce, for gold. In Abyssinia, slabs of rock salt, called "amôlés, became legal tender. Yet today, salt one of the most commonplace commodities on earth.

You might be wondering—if salt is so cheap, so plentiful, so ordinary—why did I write this section and why is it so important? Not all salts are created equal—salt isn't just salt. The seasoning that we consume is 98 percent sodium chloride; the remaining two percent is what makes the difference. That two percent contains subtle flavors and aromas imparted from the waters and surrounding minerals from which the salts are harvested. Those flavors are key to the cookies and side dish I share with you here.

Table Salt—The standard recipe salt. Fine-grained and contains anti-caking agents and (often) iodine. Use in cooking and baking, where precise measurements and table salt's consistent grain and strength are required.

Kosher Salt—The go-to salt for chefs who appreciate the lack of additives and the coarse grain (to get a "pinch"). Use it to season anything cooked in a saucepan or sauté pan. You won't need to use as much as table salt. Crystalline Sea Salt—By-product of evaporating seawater, available in fine and coarse grains, prized for its pure flavor. Use in baking (fine grain) or cooking (coarse grain).

Grey Salt—Most comes from Brittany where the clay soil lends a grey tinge. The trace minerals give it a complex flavor. Use as a finishing salt.

Fleur de Sel—Expensive and worth the cost. These crystals, like snowflakes, form on the top of salt flats and achieve a delicate texture from the breezes that blow across them. Use by sprinkling on your finest foods (such as aged steak, heirloom tomatoes, or a salad of baby greens with artisanal oil and aged balsamic vinegar) just before serving. The instant they touch your tongue they explode with flavor--think of them as Nature's pop-rocks.

Lemon Rosemary Sea Salt Shortbread Bars

<u>Ingredients</u>
1 3/4cups flour
1/4 tsp. table salt
1 tablespoon fresh lemon zest
1 tsp. fresh rosemary, finely minced
1/2 cup unsalted butter, room temperature
1 large egg
2 large egg yolks
2 tsp. water
1 tablespoon coarse sea salt

<u>Directions</u>
1) Combine the flour, table salt, zest, and rosemary in medium mixing bowl. Add the butter and cut in with pastry blender until mixture resembles coarse crumbs.

2) Blend the egg, egg yolks, and water together in a small bowl. Set aside one tablespoon of the mixture. Add the remaining egg/water mixture to the flour/butter mixture. Stir to combine and form rough dough. Turn the dough out onto a lightly-floured surface. Knead two or three times, until the dough sticks together. Press into a 1-inch thick round. Cover with plastic wrap and chill in the refrigerator for 30 minutes.

3) Preheat oven to 350 degrees F. Line a baking sheet with parchment paper.

4) Remove dough from the refrigerator, unwrap, and place on a floured surface. Pat the dough into a 6-inch by 5-inch rectangle. Using a rolling pin, roll the dough into a 10-inch by 7-inch rectangle. Cut the dough into half-inch wide strips.

5) Place the cookies on prepared baking sheet; brush the tops with the reserved egg/water mixture and then sprinkle the sea salt on top. Press the salt down so that it adheres to the cookies. Bake until golden brown, about 15 to 20 minutes.

Bruschetta with Sautéed Spinach

Ingredients
1 tablespoon plus 4 tsp. extra-virgin olive oil
1 tablespoon minced garlic
8 ounces spinach, washed, stems removed, and chopped
8 small slices artisanal bread, lightly toasted
Gray salt
Freshly ground black pepper

Directions
1) Heat 1 tablespoon olive oil in heavy large sauté pan over medium heat. Add garlic and stir 15 seconds, until fragrant. Add spinach and sauté until tender and wilted, about 3 minutes.

2) Drizzle 1/2 tsp. olive oil on each piece of toast. Top with spinach and then sprinkle with grey salt and black pepper.

THYME

"Merciless emperors and embattled soldiers, knights in shining armor and woodland fairies, the birth of a Savior and the scourge of the Black Plague—thyme, for such a delicate looking plant, you certainly have a long storied history." —Author

It is thought that the ancient Sumerians were the first to grow thyme, perhaps as long as 5,000 years ago. They recognized its minty-clove aroma as a hint to its potential for medicinal purposes and thus began the use of thyme as an antiseptic and disinfectant.

Thyme's use as a curative was continued by the Ancient Greeks and Romans. The Greeks used sprigs of thyme as a preservative for fruit and wine, and drank tinctures of it to ward off nightmares. They revered thyme as a symbol of courage and burned bundles of it as incense, the aroma purported to imbue soldiers with a spirit of fearlessness and endurance. This association of thyme and courage continued in the Middle Ages. In the days of knights, beleaguered castles, and chivalry, fair maidens would embroider scarves with sprays of thyme—the scarves to be worn by their true loves as they entered into battle.

The Romans also believed in the power of thyme to give courage to their soldiers. And they believed that the scent of burning thyme would repel scorpions.

"thyme…puts to flight all venomous creatures."— *Pliny the Elder*

In the Roman era it was also thought that ingesting thyme would protect one from poison. (I think we can assume that large beds of thyme were well-tended in the gardens of the Emperor.) Thyme was even tossed into the bathwater as an added safeguard. And it was the Romans who introduced thyme to England, where it thrived and still grows today.

Fast-forward 1,300 years. When the Black Death struck, millions of people in Europe used thyme for protection and cure. Thyme was worn around the neck, burned to fill the air with its pungent smoke, applied as a poultice to festering blistered skin, and stuffed in the masks of attending physicians.

Leave it to the Victorians to take the mythology of thyme to a whole new level. They considered a patch of wild thyme in the woods to be indisputable evidence that fairies had danced on that very spot. Perhaps we should blame that folly on Shakespeare. In ***"A Midsummer Night's Dream"***, he wrote that Titania, the Queen of the Faeries, often went to "a bank whereon the wild thyme blows." But the Victorians weren't totally clueless. Long before the control of infections was fully understood, they were soaking bandages in thyme tea.

Does thyme give one courage or prevent nightmares? Is it an antitoxin or evidence of fairy visits? Call me a cynic, but I really doubt it. However, thyme does contain *thymol*, a naturally-occurring compound with strong antimicrobial properties. In other words, it fights germs and fungus. Listerine mouth wash, anti-fungal creams, and some toothpastes and topical preparations for acne contain it. Thymol is also available as an over-the-counter product, but I'm not here to promote or endorse the use of thymol for self-medication.

I would much rather **cook** with thyme.

Europeans didn't use thyme solely to combat the plague or chase nightmares. They also recognized it as a valuable seasoning for foods. Historians tell us that monasteries maintained enviable herbal gardens. Because they were secluded and self-sufficient, the monks who lived there had to rely on their own resources when caring for their sick and injured, and they raised their own food.

Bear in mind that thyme is not meant to be the star of the show. As a member of the mint family it could overwhelm in a solo performance. But, when paired with onion, garlic, parsley, or other herbs, it lends a subtle warmth and complexity to dishes that would otherwise have just a single note. A few leaves lend an aromatic undertone that brings all other flavors into sharper focus, as in these recipes for lemon thyme risotto and roasted radishes.

Lemon Thyme Risotto

Ingredients

2 tablespoons butter
1 1/2 tsp. olive oil
1/2 cup minced onion
1/2 cup finely diced celery
1 garlic clove, minced
2 thyme sprigs or lemon thyme sprigs, leaves removed
3/4 cup dry white wine
1 cup Arborio rice
1/4 tsp. ground black pepper
3-4 cups chicken, vegetable, or mushroom broth, heated to a simmer
1/4 cup Parmigiano-Reggiano, grated
1/4 cup mascarpone cheese
Juice and zest of 1/2 lemon

Directions

1) In large frying pan melt 1 tablespoon butter with olive oil over medium heat. Add onion, celery, and garlic and cook until onion is soft, about 2 minutes. Stir in thyme. Add 1/4 cup of the wine and cook until wine is absorbed. Remove from heat and cover to keep warm.

2) Melt remaining 1 tablespoon butter in a large heavy saucepan over medium heat. Add rice, pepper, and remaining 1/2 cup white wine. Stir to insure that rice does not clump together and cook until wine is absorbed. Add 1 cup broth; reduce heat to low, and stir until broth is almost absorbed.

3) Continue to add broth, 1/2 cup at a time, stirring until rice is creamy and tender but still firm in center. (about 15 to 18 minutes). Stir in onion/thyme mixture. Remove from heat and stir in cheeses, lemon juice and lemon zest.

Roasted Radishes with Thyme

<u>**Ingredients**</u>

1 bunch (about 1 pound) assorted small radishes

2 sprigs fresh thyme

2 tablespoons olive oil

1 tablespoon butter, melted

Sea salt and freshly ground black pepper

<u>**Directions**</u>

1) Preheat oven to 400 degrees F.

2) Wash the radishes. Cut off the root ends and the tops, leaving about 1/2 inch of the stem. Dry and then transfer to a large bowl with the thyme, olive oil and melted butter.

3) Toss to combine. Place in a shallow baking dish then sprinkle with sea salt and a few grinds of pepper. Bake in preheated oven 10-15 minutes.

ONCE UPON AN ONION

BROCCOLI

"I do not like broccoli. And I haven't liked it since I was a little kid and my mother made me eat it. And I'm President of the United States and I'm not going to eat any more broccoli." –**George W. Bush**, *U.S. President*

...and with those words, every mother in America despaired of enticing her children to eat broccoli ever again.

However, a long time ago...(but not in another galaxy) *Brassica oleracea italica* was growing wild in the Mediterranean region of Europe. As the name might imply, Italy is the birthplace of the cultivar we know today as broccoli. In fact, the name broccoli comes from the Italian brocco, meaning sprout" or shoot" which, in turn came from the Latin brachium, meaning "arm" or "branch." Food historians date brassica to about 6,000 B.C.—yes, over 8,000 years ago Etruscans were cultivating wild cabbage plants. Pliny the Elder (Roman philosopher and author) wrote of them, and the Romans enjoyed a form that was purple (similar to the color of red cabbage). So, long before George Bush announced his hatred of the dreaded green veggie, Roman children were eating their broccoli.

By the 6th century B.C. the Roman Empire had gradually infiltrated Britain. With the Romans came cabbage (and its cousins kale and cauliflower), but broccoli was still an unknown. Philip Miller's Gardener's Dictionary (1731) referred to it as "Italian asparagus." A century later, Thomas Jefferson obtained packets of "exotic" seeds from friends in Europe; as a result he planted tomatoes and broccoli in his Monticello garden to accompany his salad greens. Yet, broccoli was little more than a curiosity. That all changed however when two brothers, Stefano and Andrea D'Arrigo, emigrated from Messina, Sicily to the United States of America. Stefano was the first to arrive, making his home in Boston in 1904; his brother Andrea joined him in 1911. Together they studied English, obtained engineering degrees, and even served our Nation in WWI.

After the war, they found success in operating a roadside produce stand. A quest to locate wine grape plants led Stefano to central California where he discovered fertile farmland at (pardon the pun) dirt cheap prices. With 28 acres and mail order seeds from their homeland, the brothers planted broccoli. But there was no interstate highway system at that time, so the freshly harvested produce was loaded into boxes and sent to Boston via railroad. Ultimately Stefano permanently relocated to California to take care of the production side of the business, and Andrea maintained sales on the east coast. Soon other entrepreneurs followed the brothers' lead, and agricultural production in California became a phenomenal success. Today, D'Arrigo Bros. Co. of California produces over 30,000 acres of fresh produce each year and is a leader in the industry.

Early 20th century cookbooks provide broccoli recipes that are, well let's say less than inspirational. A 1931 USDA Bureau of Home Economics publication recommends dropping the heads and stalks into lightly salted water, boiling 15 to 25 minutes, then draining and adding melted butter (or other fat) or serving with Hollandaise sauce. In 1944 the *Good Housekeeping Cookbook* was a bit bolder and suggested the addition of Parmesan cheese. We can do better than that with a luxurious broccoli and Cheddar soup and broccoli quiche.

Cream of Broccoli/Cheddar Soup

<u>Ingredients</u>
1/4 cup butter
1 large onion, chopped
3/4 cup chopped celery
1/4 cup all-purpose flour
1 pound broccoli florets
3 cups vegetable stock
1 cup milk
Salt and pepper to taste
3 ounces Cheddar cheese, shredded

<u>Directions</u>
1) Melt butter in heavy large pot over medium heat. Add onion and celery and sauté until tender, about 8 minutes. Add broccoli and sauté 2 minutes. Add broth. Cover and simmer until broccoli is tender, about 25 minutes.

2) Working in batches, transfer soup to blender and purée until smooth. Return soup to pot. Stir in milk. (Soup can be prepared 1 day ahead. Cool slightly. Cover and refrigerate.) Bring soup to simmer; season to taste with salt and pepper. Add grated Cheddar; stir gently then serve.

What you need to know about selecting, storing, and preparing fresh broccoli:

. Look for florets that are tight clusters, not like a flower about to blossom.
. Color is important; fresh broccoli heads are dark green or purple/green (depending on the variety that you select). Avoid any that are yellowed or appear damaged (bruised).
. Any attached leaves should be fresh-looking, not limp.
. To store, place broccoli in a plastic bag, removing as much of the air from the bag as possible. It will keep this way, if refrigerated, for up to 10 days.
. Do not wash broccoli until you are ready to use it.

One day in the year 2000 our younger daughter announced that she had become a vegetarian. For a meat-and-potatoes loving family this was more than a bit of a shock. How would we survive!? Well, as the "chief cook" in the household I searched online for recipes that would remove animal carcass from our diet but still provide the nutrients we need on a daily basis. And so I reluctantly became friends with tofu. This was one of the first meals I made using soy bean curd, and everyone, even my husband, loved it.

Broccoli Quiche

<u>Ingredients</u>
1 cup plus 2 tablespoons all-purpose flour
1/4 tsp. salt
1/4 tsp. baking powder
1/4 cup olive oil
3 tablespoons ice water
Non-stick cooking spray
1 medium yellow onion, finely chopped
2 cloves garlic, minced
2 tsp. olive oil
1 lb. broccoli
1 lb. firm tofu, drained
1/2 cup milk
2 tablespoons Parmesan cheese
1/4 tsp. Dijon mustard
3/4 tsp. salt
1/4 tsp. ground nutmeg
1/2 tsp. black pepper

Directions

1) Preheat oven to 425 degrees F. Combine flour, salt, and baking powder in bowl of a food processor. Pulse several times to combine. Stir together oil and water; slowly pour through feed tube with food processor running until dough forms.

2) Turn dough out onto a lightly-floured surface. Knead 10 times. Form into a small flat disk; wrap in plastic wrap and chill 20 minutes. After the dough is chilled, roll into a 12-inch circle on lightly-floured surface.

3) Gently ease into a 9-inch pie plate coated with cooking spray. Cover with plastic wrap and chill for 10 minutes. Use a fork to lightly prick the bottom of the pastry. Take a sheet of aluminum foil or parchment paper and press it into the pie plate, gently pushing it right up against the pastry. Fill the sheet of foil or parchment paper with pie weights, dried beans or even uncooked rice to hold it in place. This weight helps the pie dough hold its shape. Bake the pie pastry for 12 minutes. Remove from the oven and set aside.

4) Reduce oven temperature to 400 degrees F. Heat a large sauté pan over medium-high heat. Add the 2 tsp. olive oil; swirl to coat the bottom of the pan. Cook the onion and garlic in the oil until softened—about 2 minutes. Remove from heat and set aside. Place the broccoli pieces in a steamer basket; steam over simmering water until very tender—about 8-10 minutes. Add to onion mixture and set aside.

5) In blender or food processor, puree the tofu and remaining ingredients (milk through ground black pepper) until smooth. Add the broccoli and onions and process until smooth. Pour into pre-baked crust; bake for 35-40 minutes or until quiche is set. Allow to sit for 5 minutes before serving.

CAULIFLOWER

*"Training is everything. The peach was once a bitter almond; cauliflower is nothing but cabbage with a college education." –***Mark Twain**

If one is to interpret the dry wit of Mr. Twain, I would come to the conclusion that he admires cauliflower. And what's not to love? Move over kale; step aside acai berry. Cauliflower is our new super food, and with good reason. Unlike kale, acai, or other "health foods" cauliflower is a blank canvas; its mild unassertive taste can readily adapt to almost any flavor profile. And cauliflower is the master of disguise—it can take the place of beef or chicken in a teriyaki stir fry, be sliced into steaks and roasted, mashed like potatoes, transformed (with the magic of the food processor) into a savory rice dish, or even shaped into gluten and flour-free bread!

The legends of cauliflower are very much like those of its genetic cousins broccoli and cabbage. All three are member of the brassica family. As I explained in the history of broccoli, food historians date this plant to about 6,000 B.C.; the name cauliflower actually originated from the Latin caulis (which means cabbage) and floris (flower).

According to Texas A&M Agrilife Extension

"Cauliflower in Turkey and Egypt was mentioned in the 16th century by European writers, but it had been certainly known in those places for 1,500 to 2,000 years or more. In England in 1586 cauliflower was referred to as "Cyprus coleworts," suggesting recent introduction from the island of Cyprus. For some time thereafter, Cyprus was mentioned as the source of seed for planting in England. Cauliflower was an item on the London vegetable market as early as 1619. It was grown in France around 1600."

At about that same time, cauliflower was also being cultivated by Colonists in America. By the 18th century recipes were appearing in home cookbooks; simmering in milk or pickling and serving as a condiment were favored methods of preparation. (Let's forget about the milk bath, and I'm not a huge fan of pickles.)

With the 21st century obsession to banish carbohydrates from our daily diets, cauliflower has achieved a new popularity. Pulverize it with a food processor and it mimics rice. Or it could stand in for couscous. The following recipe is yet another innovative spin (no pun intended)—mashed cauliflower in place of potatoes.

Mashed Cauliflower

Ingredients
3 pounds of cauliflower
1/4 cup sour cream
4 tablespoons unsalted butter
Salt and pepper to taste

Directions
Trim cauliflower to remove stem and leaves; break down into florets. Place florets in steamer basket; steam over gently boiling water until very tender; about 10 minutes. Remove basket from heat and place over large bowl. Press on cauliflower with back of spoon to extract water from the cooked vegetables (yes, there will be water—lots of water). Push, push! Place 'squished" cauliflower in food processor. Add sour cream, butter, and seasonings; process until smooth. (Unlike potatoes, this mash doesn't become gluey when whipped in a food processor).

Do you want your children to eat more vegetables? I'll bet they will never notice the cauliflower hiding in this hearty macaroni and cheese dish.

Macaroni and Cheese with Cauliflower and Tomatoes

<u>Ingredients</u>
1 large head cauliflower (about 1 1/2 pounds), broken into small florets
1 15-oz. can stewed tomatoes, drained
2 tablespoons olive oil
2 tablespoons butter
2 tablespoons flour
1 cup half and half
2 cups shredded medium Cheddar cheese, divided
1 cup shredded Gouda cheese or smoked Gouda cheese
1/2 cup grated Parmesan cheese
1 tablespoon Dijon mustard
1 cup fat-free sour cream
12 oz. dry penne pasta

<u>Directions</u>
1) Preheat oven to 350 degrees F. Cook cauliflower in large pot of salted water until tender (about 10 minutes). Drain and set aside. Over medium heat in large open pan, sauté cooked cauliflower in 2 tablespoons olive oil until it begins to brown, about 5 minutes. Add drained stewed tomatoes and continue to cook for 1 to 2 minutes to meld flavors. Remove from heat; season with salt and pepper.

2) Melt 2 tablespoons butter in saucepan over medium heat. Add flour and stir one minute. Whisk in cream; cook until sauce thickens. Add 1 cup Cheddar cheese, the Gouda, Parmesan, and mustard and continue to cook until all cheese is melted and sauce is smooth. Remove from heat and whisk in sour cream; set aside.

3) Cook pasta according to package directions until al dente. Drain, and return pasta to pot. Stir in cheese sauce. Butter a large casserole dish and spoon in 1/3 of pasta mixture. Cover with one-half of cauliflower mixture and 1/2 cup of reserved cheddar cheese. Repeat the layering, finishing with 1/3 of pasta mixture. Bake uncovered in 350 degree oven until heated through and bubbling, about 30 minutes

CORN

"…pray what more can a reasonable man desire, in peaceful times, in ordinary noons, than a sufficient number of ears of green sweet-corn boiled, with the addition of salt?" –**Henry David Thoreau**, *"Walden" (1854)*

I grew up hating corn. It was one of those unfounded hates, the "I-don't-like-green-vegetables" kind of hate, born of my mother's upbringing on a farm. Mom despised corn, saying it was "pig food", and that was enough for me. Pig food.

But then one fateful afternoon I attended a friend's backyard barbecue; there were ribs and chicken, baked beans and potato salad, and fresh steamed corn dripping with melted butter. That corn—it smelled amazing—sweet, like vanilla frosting on a cupcake, and it was the most beautiful shade of sunshine yellow. I allowed my guard to slip; I picked up an ear and inhaled the intoxicating earthy-sweet aroma. I brought it to my lips and took my first bite. The bright yellow kernels popped, releasing their sugary contents which mingled with the salty butter and…I was transported to a Heavenly place. Like sex, once you've given in to the allure of corn on the cob, there's no going back.

"Sex is good, but not as good as fresh sweet corn." –**Garrison Keillor**

Maize (or sweet corn as it is commonly known) is the Number 1 cereal food in the world. Although rice and wheat are well-known staples in diets throughout the world, corn is at the top of the list. Not only is corn the primary food source in South America and Africa, but it also serves as fodder for livestock around the globe.

Archeologists believe that corn originated in the Tehuacan Valley of Mexico 7,000 years ago. But it wasn't the corn you find at your local produce stand. The corn we love today began as nothing more than a wild grass with sparse seeds clinging to a slender stalk—a far cry from the plump kernels on sturdy cobs that we now enjoy. Ancient farmers domesticated those kernels by selective breeding—they carefully chose the seeds from the largest, plumpest, sweetest maize and planted them for the next year's harvest. In time, those plants cross-pollinated and the best characteristics became dominant, resulting in the corn we now have.

Corn sailed across the Atlantic with Columbus after either his first or second exploration, but initially was little more than a curiosity, an unusual decorative plant. Eventually it was recognized as a food crop, and within less than a century was being harvested in France, Italy, southeastern Europe, northern Africa, and even into China and the Philippines. Another migration occurred in the mid-19th century. Settlers moving across the Great Plains took corn with them where it found a perfect home. By 1880 more than 62 million acres of land were dedicated to the production of corn; by 1910 that figure had climbed to 110 million.

But did you know that in the 21st century, very little of the corn grown in the United States appears on our plates as corn kernels? Over one-third is used to feed livestock, 27 percent is turned into ethanol, 13 percent is exported, and some is used in the production of plastics. Only 11 percent (**11 percent**) is devoted to food and beverage production.

With so little corn available for summer picnics, we want to insure that what goes on our plates is the best quality. I get questions, so many questions on **how to select the best corn on the cob**. Is yellow corn sweeter than white? Do silk tassels matter? Should you peel back the husk to peek at the kernels (and if you do, what are you looking for)?

Here are the answers:

How to select the best corn on the cob

Here is all you need to know—no myths, superstitions or rumors:

First, look at the silks. There is one silk for every kernel on the cob (trust me on this). The silks should be green or a pale yellow—not brown.

Next, look at the bottom of the ear—where the corn was attached to the stalk. It should be pale green like the husk. If it is brown, the ear was picked too many days ago and your corn will not be sweet. Fresh corn has a ratio of 80 percent sugar and 20 percent starch. Within just three days that ratio can shift to 20 percent sugar and 80 percent starch.

The husks should be green, not pale yellow or (worse) brown. Are there holes in the husk? If so, just walk away. Those are worm holes.

Should you shuck before you pay the bucks? Please don't. It's a rude thing to do to the merchant and certainly to the next customer who is dealing with your discarded ears of corn. Pulling back the husk tells you nothing that you won't learn from gently peeling back the top of the husk to reveal the tip of the cob of corn. If you see plump kernels and the corn has passed the other tests mentioned above, you can be assured that the entire cob is full and worthy of purchase!

Yellow vs. White? They are all the same and I dare you to do a blind taste test. You won't know the difference.

And finally, storage. If you don't cook your corn on the same day that you purchase it, store in your refrigerator with the husks and silks ON.

Now that you know how to select the perfect ear of corn, we need to find the perfect recipes. Here are three different ways to cook corn on the cob.

Perfect Corn on the Cob

Boil
1) Don't remove the husks and silks until you are ready to cook.

2) Use a pot large enough to completely submerge the corn. Fill pot with cold (unsalted) water, cover with lid, and bring to a boil over high heat. Add husked corn and cover with lid. As soon as the water returns to a boil (3 to 4 minutes), the corn is done. Remove immediately and enjoy.

Roast
1) Preheat oven to 375 degrees F.

2) Place ears of corn directly on the oven rack. Don't husk; don't remove silks. Roast for 25 minutes; remove from oven. Remove the husks and silks.

Grill
1) Remove husks and silks.

2) Tear off a sheet of aluminum foil large enough to completely enclose the corn. Spread softened butter on one side of the foil. Center an ear of corn on the buttered side. Wrap up the corn; place on the grill for 10-12 minutes, turning occasionally.

I created the next two recipes for Thanksgiving meals in my home. Perhaps a dish such as one of these appeared at the first harvest celebration.

Homemade Creamed Corn

<u>Ingredients</u>

4 cups fresh corn kernels

3/4 cup whipping cream, divided

1 tsp. salt

1 tsp. sugar

1 tablespoon corn starch

<u>Directions</u>

Put the corn in a pan; add the salt, sugar and one half cup of the cream and bring to a boil. Reduce to low. Stir cornstarch into remaining 1/4 cup cream; stir into corn mixture and continue to simmer, stirring constantly, until desired thickness is reached.

Cheesy Corn Pudding

<u>Ingredients</u>

1 1/2 cups whole milk

1/2 tsp. salt

Dash of black pepper

1/4 cup grits or polenta (not instant)

3/4 cup **homemade creamed corn** (see my recipe), or used canned

3/4 cup sharp Cheddar cheese, shredded

2 large eggs, separated **plus** 1 egg white

<u>Directions</u>

Preheat oven to 375 degrees F. Bring milk, salt and pepper to a simmer in saucepan over medium heat. Slowly add grits in a steady stream, stirring constantly to avoid lumps. Reduce heat to low and continue to stir constantly until mixture is thickened and smooth, about 25 minutes. Transfer to a bowl and set aside to cool. Puree corn in a food processor; stir into grits. Add cheese and yolks. In a large bowl beat the three egg whites until stiff peaks form. Fold beaten whites into grits mixture; pour into medium-sized casserole dish; bake in a preheated oven 30 minutes or until pudding is set and puffed.

GREEN BEANS

"Green beans or string beans as they are usually called, must be done [boiled] till very tender — it takes nearly an hour and a half."
—**Sarah Josepha Hale** *'The Good Housekeeper'' (1839)*

The above quote from ***"The Good Housekeeper"*** was obviously taken to heart by every school cafeteria cook in the 1950's and 1960's. I can still see those miserable vegetables in my mind's eye— hopelessly flaccid and purged of every molecule of chlorophyll. My mom didn't serve green beans in our home, and for that I was thankful, thinking that "limp and gray" was what green beans were meant to be. It was also about this time in American history that the side dish "Green Bean Casserole" became a fixture in every Thanksgiving Day spread. In my estimation, green beans with "cream of clump soup" didn't seem like much of an improvement over the standard lunchroom fare. And where did this odd assemblage of ingredients originate? It's time for another story.

Today we have the internet, where recipes and cooking tips for any and all imaginable foods can be found. However, once upon a time, there were few sources for the home cook. Of course there were cookbooks, but they were expensive and cumbersome. Family favorites jotted down on time-worn (and stained) note cards often gave unclear or imprecise measurements, and provided few if any directions. Here is where ingenuity and marketing genius came to the rescue—food manufacturers (General Mills, Heinz, Kraft Foods, and dozens others) produced small, inexpensive (and often free) pamphlets filled with recipes that featured their products. The Campbell Soup company produced many of these booklets—promising tasty, balanced meals for the thrifty, time-conscious housewife.

According to the Wikipedia:

The green bean casserole was first created in 1955 by the Campbell Soup Company. Dorcas Reilly led the team that created the recipe while working as a staff member in the home economics department. The inspiration for the dish was 'to create a quick and easy recipe around two things most Americans always had on hand in the 1950s: green beans and Campbell's Cream of Mushroom Soup."

Dorcas Reilly and the Campbell Soup Company were genius! It is estimated that in 2015 more than **20 million** households prepare Green Bean Casserole on Thanksgiving. Incredibly that one recipe accounts for 25 to 30 percent of the company's sale of cream of mushroom soup in the month of November.

But as you know, long before we had Thanksgiving…there were green beans. Food historians believe that the green bean (*Phaseolus vulgaris*) originated in South America. No one knows exactly when the green bean was domesticated, but seeds have been found with a Peruvian mummy, a mummy that radiocarbon dating shows to be about 7,000 years old. Christopher Columbus found green beans growing with maize (corn) plants in the New World in 1493. He collected seeds which then traveled with him across the Atlantic in his second voyage home.

The people of the Mediterranean soon learned that green beans are relatively easy to cultivate and have a short growth cycle, reaching maturity in as little as 60 days from planting. And so their popularity spread. By the 17th century they were grown throughout Greece, Turkey, and Italy."Italy" and "green beans"—those three words bring back a flood of wonderful memories. Let me tell you a story.

A warm mid-October breeze filled with the scent of rosemary and salt air; the sound of ocean waves gently lapping against the breakwater; the sun, a ball of flame, sinking into the Ligurian Sea. These were our introduction to Vernazza and how we will always remember her.

In the Autumn of 2006 my husband, daughters, and I travelled to Europe. We spent a day in Venice and several days in Maniago and Aquillia. A short drive north took us through Austria and then to Slovenia where we visited my cousins. But most of our stay was in Italy. The weather was ideal. Although our trip spanned mid-September to mid-October there was only one brief hour of rain. The days were warm, but not hot, and evenings were a balmy, shirt-sleeve temperature. Absolutely perfect. Of all the places we visited, my fondest memories are of the **Cinque Terre.**

The Cinque Terre (5 Lands) is five small coastal villages on the west coast of Italy. Monterosso, the northernmost town, is the only one that feels 'touristy". If you love the Riviera (beach, boardwalk, and luxury hotels) this is the place for you. Then there is Riomaggiore, Manarola, Corniglia, and Vernazza. These four still hold their old-world charm with narrow crooked streets, bell towers, castellos, fishing boats—and a footpath links them together. My favorite of the five towns, and the place at which we stayed, was Vernazza.

Vernazza is described in guidebooks as "a quaint little fishing village", but it's so much more than that. Colorful homes cling to the cliffs. A lovely harbor nestles under the shadows of an ancient castle. The hills are dotted with ancient olive trees and wine-producing grape vines, still tended by hand, on steeply terraced slopes. Most of all,

Vernazza is about putting aside the frantic pace, inhaling deeply, and taking life at a slower pace. We stepped off the train at Vernazza in mid-afternoon...and stepped into another world. There are no cars in Vernazza. No traffic. No horns blaring—just the pleasant sounds of people laughing and talking, and merchants bargaining with townsfolk and tourists. A gentle sloping cobblestone road leads through the center of town past storefronts and apartments. Within 10 minutes we arrived at Trattoria Gianni. Whitewashed steps led to the room we had rented for the weekend. We hastily unpacked, and then descended the steps to the plaza. Five hundred feet away was the sand, the breakwater, and a view of the sea…which becomes the ocean…and becomes forever.

As evening approached we sat at a table in the courtyard of Trattoria Gianni. Our meal began with a basket of crusty bread, and a bottle of Gianni's family wine. We asked our server for his recommendation; he said "You must try the trofie." It was love at first bite. Trofie is a free-form pasta (no machine required) most often cooked with thinly-sliced new potatoes and slender fresh green beans, all tossed with homemade basil pesto. Here is how to make Gianni's dish.

Northern Italian Pasta with Pesto

Ingredients
12 ounces troffie or penne pasta
Yukon Gold potatoes (enough to make 2 cups sliced)
Fresh green beans—again, enough to make 2 cups sliced (look for green beans that are thin and young)
About 1 cup pesto (homemade is best)
1 cup grated Parmesan cheese

Directions
Bring a large pot of water to a boil (at least 4 quarts). Drop in the potato slices and cook until almost tender—about 2 minutes. Lift out with a skimmer and set aside. Next, drop in the green beans. (Remove the stem end and cut in half—leaving the blossom end intact.) Cook about 2 minutes or until tender-crisp, remove with a skimmer and set aside. Add the pasta to the simmering water and cook according to package directions until al dente. Return the cooked potato slices and cooked green beans to the pot—wait 15 seconds, and then drain. Put the pasta/potatoes/green beans mixture back into the pot and mix with the pesto. Pour into a serving bowl and top with grated Parmesan. Toss and serve.

Northern Italy is also the home of Gorgonzola cheese and the pairing of crisp slightly sweet green beans with the sharp flavor of blue cheese seems a natural. Add olive oil for a buttery richness and walnuts for crunch and umami flavor.

Crisp Green Beans with Walnuts and Gorgonzola

Ingredients
3/4 pound whole green beans
2 tsp. good quality olive oil
1/3 cup crumbled Gorgonzola cheese (or other blue cheese)
1/3 cup chopped walnuts
Salt and pepper to taste

Directions
Trim green beans (remove stem end); steam until crisp-tender. Drain and return to pan. Add olive oil, cheese, and walnuts. Toss to coat; season with salt and pepper to taste.

KALE

"Vegetables are a must on a diet; I suggest carrot cake, zucchini bread, and pumpkin pie." **–Jim Davis** *(Garfield cartoonist)*

Stop the Madness! The stuff of every child's nightmare—the suspicious green vegetable—has invaded every corner of our lives. No matter where you go, when you dine out if it's green, it's kale.

The romaine lettuce of Caesar salad has been replaced by kale, and Popeye is no doubt gulping down canned kale in place of his beloved spinach. We are a nation obsessed with kale! Kale salad. Kale soup. Kale casseroles, chips, designer t-shirts, and (can you believe it) even **kale cake**!

Please, don't misunderstand me—I <u>love</u> kale. It has many health benefits (things called bioflavonoids, antioxidants and other terms I can't pronounce or understand). It's inexpensive and available year-round. It tastes wonderful—but I beg you, not in a smoothie, brownie, or cupcake. The current mania is turning kale into a four-letter word, the 'tofu" of the 21st century.

Please Mom! Not Kale

Consider for a moment—it isn't that long ago that kale was nothing more than the green frill that separated the rows of pork chops from the sirloin steaks at the butcher shop and now it is ubiquitous. Let's step back for a moment and rethink how to use (and not abuse) this culinary super-star. Kale isn't a recent fad. As man began farming and choosing the largest plants for propagation, wild kale/cabbage plants selectively became larger and larger, until they developed into the plants we would recognize today.

In 600 B.C. Greek philosopher Theophrastus wrote of kale in his book on plants. Ancient Greeks boiled and ate the leaves as a hangover remedy. As a variation of the theme, Cato advised eating cabbage or kale soaked in vinegar before embarking upon an evening of heavy drinking and the accepted remedy for a Roman hangover was simply (you guessed it) more kale. Pliny the Elder (Roman philosopher and author) also wrote of its medicinal properties.

By the 6th century B.C. the people named the Celts had gradually infiltrated Britain. With them came kale and its cabbage cousins. By the 5th century B.C., selective cultivation was leading to an increasingly "leafy" plant. The botanical name of the kale that we eat today is *Brassica oleracea acephala* which translates "cabbage of the vegetable garden without a head."

Until the Middle Ages, kale was the most popular vegetable in Europe. As a source of calcium and iron, it was a blessing to those who could not afford meat, and its hardy nature made it able to withstand even the harsh winters of Scotland and Ireland. Cabbage and kale, along with leeks and onions, were the main sources of food for the British Isles until the introduction of the potato.

In fact kale (known as *kail* in Scotland and *cole* in England) came to mean the meal itself—the main meal of the day and the Scot vegetable garden was commonly called a "kail garden". That "kail garden" is the perfect place to look for our first recipe. Any discussion of kale or cabbage in Britain makes me think of Colcannon. It's a meal my family loves, with a *bit of discretion*. Salty smoked pork and gobs of creamery butter are rich and indulgent, so we enjoy them as a guilty pleasure rather than a routine meal staple. I usually prepare Colcannon on St. Patrick's Day (March 17 in the United States). But at the grocers, there is always the question "I see that you are buying cabbage—are you making corned beef?" Most who meet me assume (correctly) that I'm part Irish. (If the reddish-blonde hair and green eyes are not enough of a hint, the leprechaun stature is usually a dead giveaway.) And so I go on to explain that corned beef and cabbage is an American dish. Any true Irishman, seeing such a large slab of meat on his table, would have thought that he had died and gone to Heaven.

Purchasing kale instead of cabbage is a bit healthier, and avoids the inevitable questions.

Colcannon (Irish Mashed Potatoes)

<u>Ingredients</u>
2 pounds smoked pork neck bones
1 quart water
1/2 head cabbage or 1 bunch kale (stems and ribs removed)
4 or 5 (depending on size) Yukon gold potatoes
1/2 cup milk
1/2 cup butter, divided

<u>Directions</u>
1) Place pork neck bones in crock pot (slow cooker). Cover with water and cook on low for 6-8 hours or until meat is tender (3-4 hours on high). Remove meat from cooker and set aside to cool. <u>Reserve the water in the crock pot.</u>

2) Chop cabbage into small (1 inch) dice and add to water in crock pot. Cover and cook on low one hour. Drain cabbage and set aside. When cool enough to handle, remove all bones and fat from cooked pork. Set aside.

3) Place potatoes in steamer basket in large saucepan with lid. Cover and steam over low heat until potatoes are done—a sharp knife should easily slide into the potato.

4) When potatoes are cool enough to handle remove skins; place peeled potatoes in large bowl. Mash until no lumps remain; add 1/4 cup butter, 1 tablespoon at a time until all butter is incorporated. Heat milk in microwave; add to potatoes and continue to whip until potatoes are creamy.

5) Using a large spoon stir cooked cabbage and cooked pork into mashed potatoes. Divide mixture among 4 serving bowls. Using a wooden spoon, make a well in the middle of each serving. Place 1 tablespoon of butter in each well.

I am not Italian—not even 1 percent. But my sister lived there for many years and I visited her as often as I could. And along the way I fell in love with the country, the people, and the food.

This story begins with an ordinary bowl of soup, ordered in a foreign language, in an unfamiliar place. The ingredients were simple—beans, carrots, onions, bread. But the result was anything but ordinary or simple. We were in Siena. Siena, Tuscany, Italy.

Surrounded by olive groves and the vineyards of Chianti, Siena is one of the most beautiful cities of Tuscany. Set on three hills, the city is drawn together by winding alleyways and steep steps to the Il Campo—a fan-shaped courtyard consisting of nine segments. Each segment represents a member of the Council of Nine (ruling body from 1287 to 1355) and the fan symbolizes the cloak of the Madonna, which according to fable, shelters Siena.

We arrived in town in late afternoon. There was just enough time for one tourist attraction (the Duomo), and then we were off to dinner. On the recommendation of a friend, we sought out and found Nello la Taverna.

Nello has been in business for more than 50 years. What led us there was the promise of vegetarian dishes. What makes us want to return again (and again) is the wonderful presentation of seasonal foods paired with homemade pasta. With every bite we fell in love. Until that first evening in Sienna, I had never heard of "bread soup". Really? Soup made with bread? It sounded more than a bit odd, but I was so wrong. When I returned home I was committed to replicating this wonderful dish.

Italian Bread Soup (Ribolitta)

<u>Ingredients</u>
10 oz. dry cannellini beans
1 medium onion, finely chopped
2 stalks celery, finely chopped
3 medium carrots, finely chopped
1/3 cup plus 2 tsp. olive oil, divided
1 large red tomato, diced
7 oz. Tuscan kale, tough rib removed and leaves chopped
2 cloves garlic, finely minced
1 tsp. fresh thyme
8 slices artisanal French of Italian bread, diced (see note)
Pinch red pepper flakes
Salt and pepper, to taste

<u>Directions</u>

1) Sort and wash the beans. What do I mean by sorting? Spread them out on a cookie sheet and pick through them looking for rocks, small clumps of dirt, or shriveled beans. Trust me; you don't want to have those things in your soup. Beans are not washed when they are harvested—any moisture would cause them to mold, so please wash your beans to remove field dust.

2) Next, place your washed beans in an 8-quart stockpot. Add enough water to have about 2 inches of water above the beans (about 6 cups of water). Bring to a boil over medium-high heat. Boil 2 minutes and then remove from the heat. Cover and let stand 1 hour. This soaking time will reduce the actually time the beans need to simmer and will help retain nutrients. Drain the beans and set aside.

3) In the same stock pot, sauté the onion, celery, and carrots in 1/3 cup olive oil until softened—about 5 minutes. Add the chopped tomato and sauté a few minutes more. Add the soaked drained beans and 2 quarts of fresh water. Bring to a boil over medium-high heat. Reduce heat to low; cover and simmer about 2 hours or until beans are tender. Once cooked, pour the beans and their cooking liquid into a large mixing bowl. Remove one-half of the beans and broth to a food processor and blend until smooth. Wash the stock pot and return it to the stove; heat to medium.

4) Add the garlic, thyme, and remaining 2 tsp. olive oil to the stock pot; simmer a few minutes. Stir in the kale and continue to cook a few minutes more, until the kale begins to wilt. Stir in the blended beans and broth. Bring all to a simmer over low heat. Simmer for 30 minutes.

5) Stir the bread into the soup. Continue cooking for another 30 minutes, mixing occasionally. This is a good time to check the salt and pepper too. Add the rest of the beans and broth and a pinch of red hot pepper. Mix in well. Serve warm with a bit of olive oil.

NOTE: If your bread is not dry you can slice it and bake it in the oven at low heat to dry it quickly.

ONIONS

"I crawled into the vegetable bin, settled on a giant onion and ate it, skin and all. It must have marked me for life for I have never ceased to love the hearty flavor of onions." **–James Beard**

Consider the lowly onion—sweet, crisp, pungent, tear-inducing...and indispensable. In any given part of the globe, the first instruction for the preparation of a dish is "chop one onion...."

According to World-Crops.com: *"Over 9.2 million acres of onions are harvested annually around the world. This production is grown from more than 8 million pounds of seed."* The harvest from those 9 million-plus acres translates to roughly 74.2 million metric tons of onions each year (that's about 11 kilograms or 24 pounds per person, assuming a global population of 6.9 billion)....It seems that there should be enough to go around.

On the surface, the onion is a simple plant, but the onion family (*Allium*) is large and diverse, with over 500 species. There is one thing on which we can all agree—that we cannot agree on where onions originated.

Ever since Cain and Abel there have been hunters and gatherers—those who pursue fish, fowl, or fanged beast; and those who till the soil, harvest the fruit, and gather the onions. But there was no written word when time began; written language came much later, so there is no recorded evidence of the first onions. Likewise, the tissue of onions leaves few discernible traces behind, so...archeologists and historians are left to rely on prehistoric remains and tools to form a hypothesis (which is a fancy way of saying that they take all of the information they can find and make a reasonable guess).

Some look to central Asia where wild onions still thrive today. It is known that more than 5,500 years ago the Chinese tended gardens of onions. The research of other food historians suggests that onions were first grown by the Babylonians in Iran and West Pakistan. Sumerians were the first civilization to develop a written language. Their writings (a form of hieroglyphics known as cuneiform) contain this inscription:

"The oxen of the gods plowed the city governor's onion patches. The onion and cucumber patches of the city governor were located in the gods' best fields."

Whether you hold with the theory that onions originated in Asia or came from the cradle of civilization, we can at least agree that onions would have been a staple in early man's diet. Perhaps the original fast food, onions were adaptive to many different soils and climates and so could be grown in many places. They could be stored, dried, and preserved for later use. What's not to love? And, all kidding aside, as such an important part of life, they became central to all facets of early civilization, appearing in art, medicine, and mummification. The earliest known records of the use of onions are paintings, not recipes. Around 3,200 B.C. 1st dynasty Egyptians included them in their artwork.

In Egypt, onions were more than a foodstuff; they actually became an object of worship. The Egyptians looked upon the anatomy of an onion—a circle within a circle within a circle—as a representation of eternal life. For this reason, onions were buried with the Pharaohs. (Remnants of onions have been found within the pelvic regions, chests, and ears of mummies and near the legs and soles of the feet. King Ramses IV, who died in 1,160 B.C., was buried with onions in his eye sockets!) Egyptologists theorize that onions might have been used in the mummification process as an antiseptic, or perhaps because their strong scent was thought capable of prompting the dead to breathe again.

Onions were not reserved solely for the pleasure of the wealthy Pharaohs. Apparently they were also provided to the slaves—no, not for their entombment, but for energy and strength to build the pyramids. If you have heard the story of Moses and the Israelites, you know that the Israelites fled to the Sinai Desert to escape Egyptian enslavement. While in the Sinai, they began to grumble about lack of food. In the 4th book of the Bible they complain:

"We remember the fish we ate in Egypt at no cost, and also the cucumbers, melons, leeks, **onions***, and garlic." (Numbers 11:5)*

Were onions an elixir, a source of energy, the steroid of ancient times? Alexander the Great prepared his armies for battle with (you guessed it) onions. In Greece trainees for the Olympics not only ate onions, but they also drank the juice of onions and rubbed it on their bodies as a source of energy. Romans armies ate them as well and carried them wherever they went—from Italy to Spain, Central Europe, and England. And it is from *"unio,"* the Latin word for large pearl or oneness and unity, that we derive the name onion.

According to Martin Elcort in his book *"The Secret Life of Food"*:

"The word was created by adding the onion shaped letter "o" to the word unio. A union is something that is indivisible and which, if taken apart, is destroyed in the process, like an onion"

And as Rome goes, so goes the world. With their travels (aka conquests), Roman armies introduced onions to Europe. And, what a blessing that was. After the fall of the Roman Empire, Europe plunged into what is known as the Dark or Middle Ages. The primary sources of food were beans, cabbage, and onions. Onions became not only a source of sustenance, but were also used as curatives and as a commodity. Even Charlemagne ordered that onions be planted in his royal garden.

On his second sailing to the New World, Columbus brought cultivated onions. Wild onions were growing in America, but they paled in comparison in size and intensity of flavor. It is clear that the onion has played a significant role in world affairs. The great pyramids were constructed by workers fortified by onions. The troops of Alexander the Great were sustained by onions in their conquest of what was then much of the civilized world. Ulysses S. Grant famously sent a telegram to the War Department, stating *"I will not move my army without onions."* (The next day he received three train car loads of them.)

Obviously onions need no cheerleader, but James Beard (American chef, food writer, and eccentric personality) certainly elevated the status of this root vegetable from background seasoning to star of the show. Beard's legacy lives on in twenty books, numerous writings, his own foundation, and his annual Beard awards in various culinary genres. His writing inspired me to create this flavorful onion pie.

Caramelized Onion Tart

<u>Ingredients</u>
1 tablespoon olive oil
1 tablespoon unsalted butter
1 pound yellow onions
1 pound red onions
1/2 pound cipollini
2 tablespoons fresh thyme, minced
1/2 tsp. freshly ground black pepper
1/2 tsp. salt
1/2 of a 14-oz. pkg. refrigerated pie dough
1/4 cup Feta cheese, crumbled
1/4 cup Parmesan cheese, shredded
1/4 cup crumbled Gorgonzola cheese

<u>Directions</u>
1) Preheat oven to 425 degrees F.

2) Peel the onions. Using a mandolin or the slicing blade of a food processor thinly slice the yellow and red onions. Slice the cipollini with a sharp knife. Line a baking sheet with paper towels; place the onions on the paper towels and allow to sit for about 10 minutes to remove some of the excess moisture. (Did you know that onions are 89 percent water?

3) Heat the oil and butter in a large sauté pan over medium heat. Place the onions, thyme, salt and pepper in the pan and cook, stirring occasionally about 20 minutes or until the onions are softened and begin to turn golden brown. Don't hurry the process by turning up the heat—the onions will burn and taste bitter. You want them to caramelize.

4) Line a 10-inch tart pan with the pie dough. Sprinkle feta cheese on the pastry, followed by the Parmesan and Gorgonzola cheeses. Top with the onion mixture. Bake at 425° for 25 minutes or until golden. Cool for 10 minutes.

Why Use 3 Different Onions
in the Caramelized Onion Tart?

Gertrude Stein wrote "a rose is a rose is a rose," but not all onions are created equal.

Yellow onions turn a rich, dark brown when caramelized and give French onion soup its sweet flavor. Red onions hold their shape and have a more assertive "onion-y" taste. Cipollini are tender and very sweet. So there you have it—three onions—three levels of flavor.

We can't consider cooking with onions (and French inspiration) without discussing French onion soup. Typically, when we think of French onion soup, we imagine caramelized onions slowly simmering in a rich beefy broth—not a friendly ingredient when someone you love (my younger daughter) is a vegetarian. What can you do to capture that savory taste without using animal protein? The key to the puzzle is in understanding the science of taste. There are five distinct tastes that the human tongue recognizes—sweet, sour, salty, bitter, and umami. The first four you are probably familiar with:

> **Sweet** is a pleasurable sensation produced by sugars.
> **Sour** is the detection of acidity—citrus fruits, some melons, and some unripened fruits.
> **Salty** is mostly from the presence of sodium.
> A **bitter** taste is usually deemed unpleasant or disagreeable. (black coffee)

And then there is umami. Umami is a Japanese word for "pleasant savory taste"—a MEATY taste. There are numerous non-meat foods that have a umami flavor—tomatoes, mushrooms, soy, potatoes, carrots, and Parmesan cheese are a few of them. Here is how to make a rich meaty-tasting French onion soup without beef.

French Onion Soup

Ingredients
1 tablespoon olive oil
2 1/2 pounds red onions, thinly sliced
1 tsp. salt
1/4 tsp. black pepper
1 cup dry red wine
2 tablespoons tomato paste
4 cups water
1 cup canned diced tomatoes, drained
1 tsp. fresh rosemary, minced
1/4 tsp. dried thyme leaves
2 bay leaves
1 tablespoon soy sauce
1 day-old baguette, cut into 1/2-inch thick slices
1/2 cup Parmesan, grated
1/2 cup Swiss or Gruyere, grated

Directions

1) Sauté the onions in the olive oil in a large sauté pan or Dutch oven over medium-low heat, stirring frequently, until browned—about 30 minutes. (This first step requires a bit of patience. The onions need to caramelize low and slow to develop the rich, sweet flavor one associates with French onion soup. Hurry the process with high heat and you will have bitter, burned onions. If you don't allow the onions to develop a deep golden color you'll end up with flabby, watery, and tasteless onions.)

2) Increase heat to medium-high. Add salt and pepper, wine, and tomato paste. Cook until wine is almost evaporated (about 5 minutes). Add water, tomatoes, and herbs. Bring to a boil and then cover; reduce heat to simmer and cook about 20 minutes. Stir in soy sauce. Discard bay leaves. We prefer to leave the tomato pieces in our soup, but you may strain the broth and discard the solids if you wish.

OK, now you have the **vegetarian stock**. And you can use this for so many more things than French onion soup. So, keep this recipe in your back pocket (as my dad would have said) for future reference. But, if you want to proceed to turn this into Ooey-Gooey-Cheesy-Goodness, go on to the next page.

3) Preheat oven to 350 degrees F. Brush bread slices with olive oil; place on a rimmed baking sheet and bake in oven until edges are brown, about 5 minutes. Set aside.

4) When ready to serve, whisk the 1/2 cup Parmesan into your hot broth. It's important to whisk in the cheese at the last minute, or else the cheese will fall to the bottom of the pot and burn. Ladle the hot soup into heatproof bowls, and lay a slice of the baked bread on top of each bowl. Sprinkle a layer of Gruyere cheese over the bread, and then place the crocks under the broiler until the cheese bubbles and browns.

Some foods are easily converted to "vegetarian"—others, not quite so much. One would think the chili would be an easy switch—that veggie crumbles could easily substitute for the ground beef, but I've never been satisfied with the flavor. Veggie crumbles, although wonderful in texture, just don't fit in with the flavors I expect to find in chili (they tend to be a tad sweet). So I began a quest to find something that would give us that umami flavor of beef without sacrificing a cow. Most, if not all, chili recipes already contain tomatoes. I knew that potatoes and Parmesan would not fit the standard profile. And soy has such a distinctly "Asian" connotation I knew it would not work either, but what about mushrooms? Here's how I put together a "meaty" but meatless chili which also includes (of course) onions. In this recipe I will give you detailed instructions to guide you in cooking dry beans.

"Meaty" Vegetarian Chili

<u>Ingredients</u>
1/2 cup dry pinto beans
1/2 cup dry kidney beans
1 cup dry black beans
1 28-oz. can crushed tomatoes
1 tablespoon each ground cumin, smoked paprika, and chili powder
1 tsp. dried coriander
1/2 tsp. dried oregano
1 or 2 jalapeño peppers, (remove the seeds if you want less heat)
1 lb. crimini mushrooms
1 medium carrot
1 large onion
2 stalks celery
1/4 cup olive oil
4 cloves garlic, minced
2 bay leaves
2 tsp. lemon juice

<u>Directions</u>
1) Prepare the vegetables; chop the mushrooms and finely dice the carrot, celery, and onion.

2) Next, carefully sort through the beans. Rinse well and place in a large stockpot. Add 2 quarts of water. Bring to a boil over medium-high heat. Boil for 2 minutes. Remove from heat, cover and let sit for 1 hour.

3) Drain the beans and return to the pot. Add water to cover the beans by an inch or so; bring to a boil. Simmer until the beans are very tender, 1 to 2 hours. Drain the beans, reserving 1 1/2 cups of the cooking water. Place the drained beans back in the pot and set aside.

4) Place the tomatoes, spices, and jalapenos in a blender container—blend until smooth. Set aside.

5) In a large sauté pan cook the mushrooms in 2 tablespoons of the olive oil over medium heat until they give off their water, the water evaporates, and they begin to brown. Remove from the pan and set aside.

6) Next, add the remaining oil to the pan and simmer the carrots, onion, and celery over medium heat until the vegetables are soft—about 10 minutes.

7) Add the garlic and bay leaves and sauté one minute more. Add the tomato/spice mixture, the sautéed mushrooms, and the sautéed vegetables to the stock pot of beans. Stir in 1/2 cup of reserved cooking water.

8) Simmer over low heat until heated through and the flavors are blended—about 15 minutes. Add more of the reserved cooking water if needed to prevent burning. Remove the bay leaves. Stir in the lemon juice. Taste for salt and pepper and season accordingly.

The Onion Family

White Onions

White onions have an all-white skin and flesh. They are slightly milder in flavor than the yellow onion and are a great substitute if you're in need of an onion flavor, but don't want it to be too powerful.

Red Onions

These beauties have purple outer skins and red flesh. They are similar in taste to yellow onions. Because of their color they are often used raw in salsas and salads. If you find that the flavor of red onions is too sharp, but you want to use them for their color, soak slices in water before preparing.

And Even More Onions!

Green Onions

Also known as scallions; they usually have a mildly pungent flavor Scallions are long, with a white stem end that does not bulge out. They have an onion-y but mild bite that is not as intense as regular onions (the white parts contain the most intense flavor). They can be used raw or cooked, and while some cooks discard the darker green tops, the whole thing can be eaten, and is often used in Asian cooking. Scallions are usually available year-round. Look for a bright color, undamaged leaves, and firm stem ends.

Leeks

Like shallots, leeks are easy to grow, yet inexplicably expensive to buy at the grocery store. When small, they can be harvested like green onions. Plant them in a deep trench and mound soil around them as they grow. This "mounding" will keep the bottom of the plant from turning green. In about 120 days, when the plants are 1-inch or more in diameter, you may harvest your leeks; you will be rewarded with snow-white, tender stalks. Leeks have a mellow flavor and can be used in place of yellow onions.

Shallots

Shallots have a mild, delicate flavor and are simple to grow at home, but (oddly) are quite expensive. They have mild but distinctive flavor that is amazing in soups and sauces.

CONCLUSION

I began "writing" this book over 60 years ago. It started with curiosity—watching my mother and sister working in the kitchen. Cookbooks sat on the shelf but I never saw them being used. It seemed that every measurement, every action was known, memorized, and almost involuntary. Our meals were simple, but they were nourishing, comforting, and I knew instinctively that they were handed down from the previous generation to our own. I knew that the food my mother made for us was a piece of her childhood, and of the children before her, and so on, and so on.

When we share our recipes, we share not only our traditions and backgrounds—we share the memories that formed us and make us who we are. My purpose in writing this book was twofold—first, that you would enjoy and learn from the stories I shared, and second, that you would go on to create food memories of your own.

INDEX

BEANS
Italian bread soup 103
"Meaty" vegetarian chili 112

BREAD
Bruschetta with sautéed spinach 77
French toast with caramelized pears and brie 39
Italian bread soup 103
Lemon blueberry cream scones 32
Pear Crostini with blue cheese and honey 38
Pumpkin spice scones 55
Rosemary focaccia 68

BREAKFAST/BRUNCH
Broccoli quiche 86
French toast with caramelized pears and brie 39
Joes special 64
Lemon blueberry cream scones 32
Turkey breakfast sausage patties 72

BROCCOLI
Broccoli quiche 86
Cream of Broccoli/Cheddar Soup 85
How to select, store, prepare 85

CABBAGE
Chicken Waldorf tarragon salad 21

CAULIFLOWER
Macaroni and cheese with cauliflower and tomatoes 90
Mashed cauliflower 89

CELERY
Chicken Waldorf tarragon salad 21
Rosemary chicken salad sandwich 27

CHEESE, BLUE
Caramelized onion tart 108
Creamy blue cheese sauce 5
Crisp green beans with walnuts and Gorgonzola 99
Pear Crostini with blue cheese and honey 38
Potato gnocchi with gorgonzola sauce 7
Triple tomato soup 6

CHEESE, BRIE
Brie and fruit 10
Brie in puff pastry 10
French toast with caramelized pears and brie 31

CHEESE, CHEDDAR
Cheesy corn pudding 95
Cream of broccoli/cheddar soup 85
Macaroni and cheese with cauliflower and tomatoes 90
Slow-roasted tomato tart 43

CHEESE, PARMESAN/ROMANO
Broccoli quiche 86
Caramelized onion tart 108
French onion soup 110
Joes special 64
Lemon thyme risotto 80
Macaroni and cheese with cauliflower and tomatoes 90
Mushroom risotto 16
Northern Italian pasta with pesto 99
Pasta with pepper and Pecorino Romano cheese 51
Spring harvest pesto 14

GINGER
Florence's slice and bake spice cookies 59
Orange ginger prawns 58
Pumpkin spice scones 55
Turkey breakfast sausage patties 72

GREEN BEANS
Crisp green beans with walnuts and Gorgonzola 99
Northern Italian pasta with pesto 99

HAZELNUTS
Hazelnut-crusted salmon with dried cranberries 28

HONEY
Pear Crostini with blue cheese and honey 38

KALE
Colcannon (Irish mashed potatoes) 102
Italian bread soup 103

LEMON
Chicken picatta 35
Lemon blueberry cream scones 32
Lemon glaze 32
Lemon mayonnaise 21
Lemon meringue pie 33
Lemon rosemary sea salt shortbread bars 76
Lemon thyme risotto 80
Pasta with pepper and Pecorino Romano cheese 51
Velvety lemon chicken soup 31

MAIN DISH
Broccoli quiche 86
Caramelized onion tart 108

MAIN DISH (continued)
Chicken picatta 35
Colcannon (Irish mashed potatoes) 102
French onion soup 110
Italian bread soup 103
Joes special 64
Macaroni and cheese with cauliflower and tomatoes 90
"Meaty" vegetarian chili 112
Mushroom risotto 16
Northern Italian pasta with pesto 99
Orange ginger prawns 58
Pasta with pepper and Pecorino Romano cheese 51
Potato gnocchi with gorgonzola sauce 7
Warm cioppino salad 42

NUTMEG
Florence's slice and bake spice cookies 59
Joes special 64
Scallop chowder 63

NUTS
See specific type

OLIVES
Warm Cioppini salad 42

PASTA
Macaroni and cheese with cauliflower and tomatoes 90
Northern Italian pasta with pesto 99
Pasta with pepper and Pecorino Romano cheese 51
Potato gnocchi with Gorgonzola sauce 7
Spring harvest pesto 14

PEARS
French toast with caramelized pears and brie 39
Pear Crostini with blue cheese and honey 38

PORK
Colcannon (Irish mashed potatoes) 102

POTATOES
Colcannon (Irish mashed potatoes) 102
Northern Italian pasta with pesto 99
Potato gnocchi with gorgonzola sauce 7
Scallop chowder 63

RICE
Lemon thyme risotto 80
Mushroom risotto 16
Wild rice spinach salad with cranberries 26

ROSEMARY
Chicken salad sandwich 27
French onion soup 110
Lemon rosemary sea salt shortbread bars 76
Rosemary focaccia 68
Rosemary shortbread cookies 70

SAGE
Triple tomato soup 6
Turkey breakfast sausage patties 72

SALAD
Bread salad (panzanella) 48
Chicken Waldorf tarragon salad 21
Warm cioppino salad 42

SALMON
Hazelnut-crusted with dried cranberries 28

SANDWICH
Rosemary chicken salad 27

SEAFOOD
Orange ginger prawns 58
Scallop chowder 63
Warm cioppino salad 42

SOUP
Cream of Broccoli/Cheddar Soup 85
French onion soup 110
Italian bread soup 103
Scallop chowder 63
Triple tomato soup 6
Velvety lemon chicken soup 31

SPINACH
Bruschetta with sautéed spinach 77
Joes special 64
Wild rice spinach salad with cranberries 25

TARRAGON
Chicken Waldorf tarragon salad 21
Hazelnut-crusted salmon with dried cranberries 28

THYME
Cider-braised turkey thighs 23
French onion soup 110
Italian bread soup 103
Lemon thyme risotto 80
Roasted radishes with thyme 81

THYME (continued)
Slow-roasted tomato tart 43
Turkey breakfast sausage patties 72

TOFU
Broccoli quiche 86

TOMATOES
Bread salad (panzanella) 48
Italian bread soup103
Macaroni and cheese with cauliflower and tomatoes 90
Slow-roasted tomato tart 43
Triple tomato soup 6
Warm cioppino salad 42

TURKEY
Cider-braised turkey thighs 23
Turkey breakfast sausage patties 72
Wild rice spinach salad with cranberries 26

WALNUTS
Crisp green beans with walnuts and Gorgonzola 99
Spring harvest pesto 14

VEGETARIAN
Bread salad (panzanella) 48
Brie and fruit 10
Brie and puff pastry 10
Broccoli quiche 86
Bruschetta with sautéed spinach 77
Caramelized onion tart 108
Cheesy corn pudding 95
Cream of broccoli/cheddar soup 85
Creamy blue cheese sauce 5

VEGETARIAN (continued)
Crisp green beans with walnuts and Gorgonzola 99
Florence's slice and bake cookies 59
French onion soup 110
French toast with caramelized pears and brie 39
Homemade creamed corn 95
Homemade vegetarian stock 111
Italian bread soup 103
Lemon blueberry cream scones 32
Lemon meringue pie 33
Lemon rosemary sea salt shortbread bars 76
Lemon thyme risotto 80
Macaroni and cheese with cauliflower and tomatoes 90
Mashed cauliflower 89
"Meaty" vegetarian chili 112
Mushroom risotto 16
Northern Italian pasta with pesto 99
Pasta with pepper and Pecorino Romano cheese 51
Pear Crostini with blue cheese and honey 38
Perfect corn on the cob 94
Potato gnocchi with Gorgonzola sauce 7
Pumpkin spice scones 55
Roasted radishes with thyme 81
Rosemary Focaccia 68
Rosemary shortbread cookies 70
Slow-roasted tomato tart 43
Spring harvest pesto 14
Triple tomato soup 6

ABOUT THE AUTHOR

Linda Lum has been creating original foods—fusions of old and new, customs and cultures—for over 40 years. Although an avowed Italophile (lover of all things Italian), she enjoys using the flavors of all cuisines in her cooking. Linda's recipes have appeared in *Better Homes and Gardens, Cooking Light, and Sunset* magazines and have received Honorable Mention in contests sponsored by Progresso Soups and Sutter Home Wines. She is a regular contributor to Delishably.com under the name Carb Diva. Linda lives in the Puget Sound area of Washington State with her husband and two daughters.

69793159R00074

Made in the USA
Columbia, SC
22 April 2017